Contents

PART ONE: ANOTHER APPROACH
1. Introduction 3
2. Realism 3
3. Taking Disarmament Seriously 7
4. An Alternative Foreign Policy 8
5. Objectives 9

PART TWO: SOME PROPOSALS
6. The Quest for Strategic Stability 11
7. No First Use of Nuclear Weapons 12
8. The Targeting of Weapons and the Protection of Non-Combatants 14
9. The Problem of Tactical Nuclear Weapons 16
10. The Testing of Weapons 17
    A Comprehensive Nuclear Test Ban 17
    Flight Testing 18
11. Geographical Restrictions 18
    Nuclear-Weapon-Free Zones 18
    Zones of Peace 18
12. Controls on Nuclear Proliferation 19
13. Conventional War: Arms Transfers and Regional Agreements 21
14. Confidence-Building and Peace-Keeping 23
15. War Crimes and Personal Accountability 24
16. General and Complete Disarmament 26

MIL
JX
1974
.R29

MILITARY
COLLECTION

WIDENER COLLEGE
WOLFGRAM
LIBRARY
CHESTER, PA.

163730

Institute for Policy Studies
Issue Paper

Toward World Security:
A Program for Disarmament

by Earl C. Ravenal
with Richard Barnet, Robert Borosage, Michael Klare, and Marcus Raskin

JX
1974
.R29

Part One: Another Approach

1. Introduction

Disarmament has been with us as an ideal for centuries. Specific proposals for disarmament, more or less the same, have abounded for at least the past two decades. Yet wars proliferate; nations, large and small, increase their military budgets; the nuclear balance is reset at higher levels of terror; people live in fear; and their cities rot, their lives are stunted, and their dreams—which could be bought with a fraction of what the world wastes on war and the preparation for war—languish.

Moreover, we are living in a situation that has strong resemblance to the years before World War I: competitive armaments, regional antagonisms and irredentisms that provide pretexts for aggression and conflict; unstable alliance systems opposing each other across still tentative borders; profound social unrest and unmet domestic problems; the danger of mobilization and counter-mobilization, though now in the form of nuclear escalation. In such a climate, in 1914, "prudent" deterrent moves did not prevent war; they precipitated, accelerated, and expanded it.

For these reasons, the nations of the world have an urgent and objective interest in a new approach to disarmament—an interest that they cannot deny or alienate, even by their negligent and irresponsible conduct. In fact, it is the wealthiest, the most "powerful," nations—preeminently the United States—that have the greatest interest in a substantially disarmed, and particularly a non-nuclear, world, since they have the most to lose, not just through their involvement in the regional quarrels of other nations, but through their vulnerability to blackmail by nationalist and non-national terrorists.

We do not believe that there is a shortage of specific proposals for disarmament, or that people don't want peace enough to seize it. The poor political prospects for disarmament now, and the lack of public understanding and support, reflect intellectual and educational failures. The logical basis for disarmament is not clear. Past arguments are out of touch with current international circumstances, and have been overtaken by technology.

This belief frames the intention of the paper. It will not provide a comprehensive listing of schemes; it will incorporate a good many of other people's proposals that are sensible and pragmatic. It will not offer any new gimmicks; one would have to reach far to find any, after twenty years of draftsmanship and bargaining. Our presentation will be marked by three characteristics: (1) realism, (2) a commitment to substantive disarmament, and (3) the encompassing objective of a new approach to world security through an alternative American foreign policy.

2. Realism

What, specifically, has been wrong with disarmament efforts over the past two decades?

First, they have too often assumed a universal international organization—virtually a world government—with the subordination of nation-states and the attainment of security through a central police force. The fault has been to discount the stubborn longevity of the nation-state, and the probability that disarmament efforts for the next half-century will take place in a world of nation-states. True, most nation-states may be porous and incompetent; but they are nevertheless the source of foreign policy decision-making for the foreseeable future. That fact alone makes it imperative to redefine "general and complete disarmament," even while seriously espousing it, to conform to a fragmented international system. We cannot premise a realistic approach to disarmament on the utopia of an effective, universal, supranational organization.

This need not be an occasion for despair. Impressive measures of peace have been achieved within the context of independent nation-states. Nations have, in the past, negotiated stringent limits on arms, and have actually destroyed considerable stores of their own major military equipment (viz. the Washington Naval Treaties of 1922 that limited the battleships of the five great naval powers). They have also devised serious restraints on the conduct of war (viz. the Hague treaties around the beginning of the 20th Century, and the Geneva Conventions between

---

Our presentation will be marked by three characteristics: (1) realism, (2) a serious commitment to substantive disarmament, and (3) the encompassing objective of a new approach to world security through an alternative American foreign policy.

---

the World Wars). Nations have even agreed to outlaw war entirely as an instrument of policy, as in the Treaty of Paris (the "Kellogg-Briand Treaty") of 1928, an advance in international precedent despite its present eclipse by the proponents of Realpolitik. And, it should not be forgotten, nations for long periods of time have had very low levels of armaments, by present standards—from one-tenth to one-twentieth of what they maintain now.

Second, past disarmament proposals assumed that progress will come only through multilateral or bilateral bargaining and formal agreements among nations. Draftsmanship and legalism have been emphasized. This ignores the potential of independent, national, informal moves to disarm and to defuse the potential of war. In many important areas of disarmament, the only effective moves might be independent. Certainly we should not put all our eggs in the basket of SALT (the formal bilateral strategic arms limitation talks between the United States and the Soviet Union) or in the councils of the United Nations. We should adopt a multi-*level* approach, including multilateral, bilateral, national, and transnational forums and measures. Peace doesn't have to be formal, binding, comprehensive, or neat. It can, should, and must be achieved in patches, wherever and however possible.

We don't need protocol, draftsmanship, architectonics. We need instruments and action, concrete moves. Some, of course, will be bilateral exercises in formal "arms control," such as SALT. But formal arms control, though ideally it could resolve most of the major problems of arms proliferation and strategic instability, is not likely to do so. We are not even likely, in the next few rounds of SALT, to exact from the Soviet Union sufficient cuts in their arsenal of heavy, increasingly accurate, MIRVed intercontinental ballistic missiles (their SS-18s) to protect our own fixed land-based missiles (Minutemen). And the Soviets, on their part, will be unable to reverse the United States' formidable capability for counterforce strikes. The Carter administration tried to float such an arms reduction agreement in

In many important areas of disarmament, the only effective moves might be independent.

Moscow in March 1977; but the Soviets claimed that the United States was seeking unfair advantage—trying to disarm the Soviet Union through the strategic arms bargaining process—and indignantly rejected the U.S. proposal. As a result, the Carter administration has fallen back on a slightly tighter version of the Vladivostok limits negotiated by the Ford administration with Brezhnev in November 1974, with several additional sets of interlocking limits on offensive nuclear weapons.

Even if SALT II is signed and ratified—and we urge that this be done—it will not solve our strategic problem—notably the problem of restoring strategic stability. It will fail to do this precisely because it will not sufficiently reduce the incentives on both sides to start a nuclear war under certain crisis circumstances. Once again, as in the late 1950s, the "balance of terror" is becoming "delicate." That is one reason why we are at the edge of a critical and dangerous phase of arms competition—a counterforce race. And that is precisely why we face the need to hedge against the insufficiency of the SALT negotiations by making certain independent moves that are within our own competence—such as phasing out our land-based missiles over the next five or ten years, as they become vulnerable to improvements in Soviet accuracy and throw-weight and MIRVs. (This, and other suggestions, will be detailed below in the section on independent initiatives to restore strategic stability.)

The forums for disarmament should include multilateral ones, such as the United Nations Special Session on Disarmament in May and June 1978. The United Nations, despite its malfunctions, has a useful—even essential—role to play in the area of arms reduction. Partial multilateral conferences and organizations, such as the "club" of nuclear powers, or the suppliers of nuclear facilities and technology, or the countries of a particular region, can also play a useful role. For some disarmament moves, the most appropriate forum will be the arena of national decision-making—in short, independent moves. Finally, transnational, non-governmental institutions will be needed in any comprehensive scheme of disarmament, to prepare a receptive climate for serious reductions and other initiatives. Some initiatives, indeed, must come from such non-national groups as professional associations (scientific, legal, and other), religious groups, and other organizations that might put restraints on national governments.

In addition to working in all forums, we must work in all *areas* of arms activity: strategic nuclear weapons, tactical nuclear weapons, "peaceful" nuclear technology, conventional arms and arms transfers including instruments of repression.

Finally, we must control warlike activity in all the various *ways* that are available: quantitative limits on numbers of weapons or total explosive power; qualitative restrictions on features of weapons systems, and on research, development, and testing; non-proliferation safeguards such as inspection and monitoring of nuclear materials and facilities; geographical restrictions such as nuclear-weapon-free zones or general zones of peace; limits on military budgets; doctrinal changes (for example, no first use of nuclear weapons, and limitations on targeting and other attempts to spare non-combatants); legal strictures that reinforce personal accountability and help alter attitudes toward military actions and preparations.

A third problem with past disarmament proposals is that heavy emphasis has been placed on reducing numbers, with the implication that aggregate numbers, in themselves, cause instability and war (in a curious way the mirror-image of the hawks, who think that numbers win or lose wars). We must begin with the question: How do wars, particularly nuclear wars, start? This raises, in turn, the question of incentives: Why would either side want to start a war or escalate to the first use of nuclear weapons? What would have to be the scenario, the antecedent moves, the impending situation? To have a war, someone must have an incentive, in the particular circumstances, to use nuclear weapons first. In reverse, nations, and ultimately peoples, must have incentives to disarm. At least there must be, at all stages, the absence of overwhelming fears for their own security. Each stage of disarmament—both the end-state and the intermediate stages—must be more secure than what would otherwise be the state of affairs. Our proposals must not simply reduce forces or juggle institutions. They must create multiple and overlapping incentives and assurances to prod and allow nations to disarm.

Fourth, most peace proposals have stressed trust and good will, as if those were the primary—or even the only—factors lacking. Those who fervently desire peace often become disillusioned with the arid complexities of the contemporary arms debate. They look for some Gordian knot to cut with an immediate and comprehensible stroke of exhortation. But trust and good will are not enough. Trust must be founded on the technical and logical conditions of strategic stability. Just as lack of understanding can impede efforts to control arms, strategic instability can raise suspicions and undermine political confidence and good will. Technological factors underlie the stability of the strategic nuclear balance, particularly. In fact, in a nuclear age, strategic stability is virtually synonymous with peace. Therefore, the peace people have to be as expert as the hawks; they have to do their homework, to be able to hold their ground in debates that turn on technical characteristics and effects of weapons.

New technology has made the nuclear balance brittle again, and has brought calculations of counterforce into fashion. In certain crisis situations, counterforce strikes could be considered "productive." (Perhaps these situations are rare and even hypothetical, but the calculation of hypothetical nuclear exchanges can determine the outcome of confrontations at lower levels of escalation.) This has allowed some people, once again, to speculate about "limiting damage," even about "winning" a nuclear war by the numbers.

For a decade and a half, in a situation now castigated by many as "Mutual Assured Destruction," or "MAD," there was effective mutual vulnerability. With dispersed single-warhead missiles on each side, and with relatively low accuracies, combined with relatively low throw-weights and yields, the advantage lay with the defender, or the retaliator. It would have cost an aggressor too many missiles to take out too few of his opponent's force. He could *lose* by starting a nuclear war (in a sense even more obvious than the fact that "no one wins"). Now, with MIRVs, and with more precise accuracies, greater throw-weights, and higher yields, the advantage has reverted to the attacker, and first counterforce strikes are again, in certain situations, at least thinkable.

So we are again in an era of instability. Both sides have begun to develop and deploy potent, de-

---

To have a war, someone must have an incentive, in the particular circumstances, to use nuclear weapons first. In reverse, nations, and ultimately peoples, must have incentives to disarm.

---

stabilizing counterforce weapons (the Soviet SS-18; the U.S. Minuteman III with MK-12A warheads, and the possible follow-on MX missile). Regardless of subjective "intentions," the structure of objective incentives is again being warped, and it is being warped by technology. Therefore, to repair the situation, it will require tangible corrections—reductions and changes in weapons and force structures—not just expressions of good will.

Misplacing the problem will lead to misconceiving the answer. Many are quick to cry "pathology" or "malevolence," as if this dismisses the problem. But pathology does not fully explain the behavior of national leaderships. Though they have often traduced the desires of their constituents in the name of "national security" or "the national interest," generally leaders and policy-makers are, in a recognizable sense of the word, prudent and rational. Some day, no doubt, the present accumulation and use of arms will be regarded as madness. But it is madness of a very special kind. It has to do with the convoluted, but genuine, quest for "national security." It is the madness of the "responsible" people. Therefore, "curing" individuals, even if this were possible or likely, would not be an effective remedy. Disarmament proposals must treat "national security" as a logical and real problem, not a baseless aberration.

Fifth, many proposals for disarmament ignore the range of their possible effects. Many of them assume that all the results of disarmament would be favorable, that they would lead to peace and order and justice at the same time. Unfortunately, the choices may be harder than that. Disarmament is worth the struggle, but it will not bring all good things in its train. There may be trade-offs.

The restraint of nuclear weapons by some nations (particularly the principal "guarantor" nations) may encourage the proliferation of nuclear arms throughout the international system. Restraints on transfers of conventional arms may lead to the development of national arms production capabilities. Abolition of the "alliance system" may lead to the acquisition by other nations of independent means of defense—to a "gaullist" world. The United States may lose its influence on the choices of other nations and have to resign itself to accepting other regimes, the bad along with the good, forfeiting the ability even to bring about "justice," in some situations in the world, by intrusion or coercion. Thus, the benefits of disarmament—even the overriding benefit of more peace in the world, or at least less involvement by the United States in wars—must be described as a *net* benefit.

In making the case for disarmament, this paper aims to be tough-minded and responsible. But we take these terms in a somewhat different way: "Tough-minded" has nothing to do with the attitude of the hawks; it means being honest about the trade-offs and the balance of risks. And "responsible" has nothing to do with the compromised and stultified positions of the foreign policy establishment; it means accepting the consequences of our own proposals.

No serious business will be done on disarmament unless we identify and acknowledge the full range of possible consequences and make the hard choices. There might well be "losses," even in the "strategic" dimension, in the traditional objects of a nation's foreign and military policy, the classic stuff of the "national interest": allies, geographical positions, assured access to resources.

Indeed, our approach to disarmament, which relies on independent national actions to establish momentum within a framework of multilateral arrangements, especially risks these effects. Restraints and rules of law, if they are accepted by and enforced upon one's own government without reciprocation by others, may lead to a more disorderly and lawless world—at least for an interim period. Within a system of autonomous nation-states, disarmament may lead to disorder.

A world of diffused power, with scope for independent political initatives, would not necessarily be more conservative of existing institutions or, for that matter, more revolutionary. But political change, even of a revolutionary nature, could be conducted within the compartments with less threat of external intervention.

But there are some mitigating considerations. Disorder can be "contained," not by counterrevolutionary interventions (as the current conventional wisdom would have it), but by the very fact of a more compartmentalized world, in a political and strategic sense. A world of diffused power, with scope for independent political initiatives, would not necessarily be more conservative of existing institutions or, for that matter, more revolutionary. But political change, even of a revolutionary nature, could be conducted within the compartments with less threat of external intervention. In this way, a relatively stable and benign international system could be the overall framework for vigorous movements toward social justice in various countries. In this sense, stability should not require intervention.

The consideration of disarmament requires that we understand "national security" and "national interests" in a very different way. It isn't our object to engage in a battle of definitions; but "security" has several dimensions. It includes a productive economy and a sound society. Even the hawks recognize that these elements are related to the more classic external political-military notion of security in several ways. If economic structures are unproductive, and if society is not wholesome, foreign policy outputs are impaired. We can't generate sufficient domestic support for the necessary level of defensive effort, whatever that is, and we can't attract the allegiance of other nations on the basis of their admiration of and affinity to our example. Over the past thirty years, America has squandered the domestic economic and social materials of its security in the effort to extend its external political-military reach—an effort that, in any case, has been brought to frustration.

On the other hand, the relationship between domestic and external security is not symmetrical. A functioning economy and a sound society are necessary to maintain a constructive role and a safe place in the world; but they are clearly not sufficient. To put it crudely, we can't always substitute subway systems for aircraft carriers. This point must be acknowledged; but it need not be exaggerated, as the hysteria-mongers have been doing for a number of years. And acknowledgement does not even require that we have the aircraft carriers, or any other specific item of military hardware. It simply means that we can't use explicit "transfer" arguments, however appealing, as if they were self-sufficient, whether they are domestic social transfers or international development transfers. This remains true even though a one percent cut in the military budgets of the advanced states would fund a twenty percent increase in economic assistance to the underdeveloped countries.

In short, two cases must be made independently: disarmament, and social justice. We have to answer directly the basic questions: (1) What do we need, and for what? and (2) if we are disposed to favor social welfare or social justice at home or abroad, what can we do without? There may well be some "security risks" in preferring welfare and justice, even though welfare and justice are themselves components of "security." What we must determine is that the risks are manageable—either they are containable, or there are second chances—and that they are worth taking. What is clear is that the opposite course has been disastrous, abroad as well as at home, and that a change, accepting all the risks of a change, is long overdue.

A further word is in order about "the national interest." There can be no national interest apart from the interests of a nation's citizens—individuals and groups. This raises a question of the *identity* of the national interest. First of all, the "we" that is traditionally invoked by elites must be taken apart. And second, the real common denominator must be found in the confusing signals given off by the public. By and large, if faced with a stark choice, citizens don't want to risk being consumed in a nuclear fireball or poisoned by radioactive debris, in order to enhance their government's influence on the conduct of other nations. This elemental political fact should be binding on the decisions of policy-makers, and it should underpin all discussions of disarmament. People in all countries, ordinary citizens, tend to make different choices from their leaders; even if, in some cases, a majority would make the same war-prone choices, the contrary desires of significant minorities should count, given the extreme stakes.

By and large, if faced with a stark choice, citizens don't want to risk being consumed in a nuclear fireball or poisoned by radioactive debris, in order to enhance their government's influence on the conduct of other nations.

In sum, people don't want to be "defended" in the ways that their leaders have chosen for them. In certain extreme situations, many would secede, if they could, from the consequences of their leaders' decisions.

We are trying to put forward a disarmament program that is appropriate to the real conditions of the future international system, and that will make those conditions favorable to the continuation of human life and civilization. Such a program would seem to be realistic, in the most precise as well as the most fundamental sense. Nevertheless, the very proposal of substantial disarmament is so far from the present agenda of the principal nations that it courts charges of *un*realism, extremism, and irresponsibility.

But there is such a thing as the extremism of the center, the ultimate irresponsibility of the sober elites. All too commonly it is said that the circumstances of the nuclear age have discredited the civilized values that have painfully evolved over centuries. But those values lead to survival; and unless language has lost its meaning, the "statesmanship" that has been developed to suit a nuclear age has been precisely contrary to the probability of human survival in a nuclear age.

In putting forth these proposals for disarmament, we are not negligent of the "risks." But there is a *choice* of risks, and we should not be afraid to make our commitments and investments on the side of peace.

3. Taking Disarmament Seriously

We have said that the formal, bilateral "arms control" process is stalled, far short of effective curtailment of international violence and mass destruction. The results of arms control may have been impressive as negotiating achievements, a testimony to the energy and dedication of its proponents. But they have led, not to arms reduction, but to less restrictive ceilings and higher arms budgets; not to a reversal of the arms race, but to its diversion into qualitative improvements; not to a cooperative search for controls, but to the construction of bargaining chips; not to the relaxation of tensions, but to new occasions for recriminations and accusations of cheating. Thus, the deeper problem with "arms control" is that it is not synonymous with disarmament. Indeed, arms control was devised, fifteen or twenty years ago, to some extent to defuse pressures for more comprehensive disarmament.

This challengeable record does not mean that we should oppose partial measures of arms limitation or denigrate entirely the use of the formal bargaining context and the effort to involve our global competitors in binding treaties and cooperative undertakings. It does mean that the arms control process—formal, explicit bargaining of arms limits, with reciprocity and a good deal of symmetry as necessary conditions for any progress—must be supplemented, backstopped, by initiatives in other forums, including non-governmental transnational measures and independent actions carried out by and within individual nations. And it does mean that arms control must be transcended. Substantive and extensive arms reductions must be reinstated—as a goal, and as a proximate objective.

The last significant interest in disarmament, as distinguished from arms control, was in the early 1960s. The McCloy-Zorin "Joint Statement of Agreed Principles" of September 1961 and the U.S. and Soviet draft treaties of 1962 were the high-water mark of the movement toward general and complete disarmament.* These statements and drafts constitute useful precedents, some evidence of an

---

*There was a brief resuscitation in the 1970 Comprehensive Programme of Disarmament, which the General Assembly of the UN called to the attention of the Conference of the Committee on Disarmament (CCD). And, of course, there is the UN Special Session on Disarmament, May-June 1978, which has been the occasion for a revival of interest in substantive disarmament as well as for the submission of concrete proposals of arms limitations.

underlying will of nations to countenance comprehensive disarmament, and even a glimpse of the technical feasibility of this achievement. But, on the other hand, they must be seen as largely hypothetical schemes, intellectual concessions, with no real strategic intent—a warning to contemporary disarmament strategists that a simple return to these formulas of fifteen years ago could mean another exercise in finely crafted illusions.

A coherent strategy would reintegrate arms control and disarmament. These elements are not necessarily incompatible, if they are held in a proper mutual perspective. But both arms control and disarmament need to be restated. Arms control should be viewed as a series of staged and partial steps toward comprehensive disarmament; "resting points," each of which offers a chance to establish stability, political acceptance, and mutual confidence before moving to the next stage. General and complete disarmament should be seen as a goal; but not only that—it must also be seen as a reason for accomplishing the steps of arms control, and a standard against which one can measure each interim arms control move, to see whether, even if valid in itself, it also leads to total practicable disarmament.

Putting interim arms limitations in the context of more comprehensive disarmament raises the question of phasing. It implies the setting of stages that will form a cumulative and progressive program; stages that will each be stable and balanced, with minimum risks; and stages at which confidence can be strengthened, difficulties can be corrected, details can be filled in, and implementation can be tested. There must be time limits—definite times assigned to the attainment of the stages, not for the sake of rigidity, but to illustrate how the interim moves will create momentum toward the objective of general and complete disarmament. Ironically, the stages must be arranged so we *can* stop at any point, on any plateau, with a sense that the chances of war and the probable severity of war are diminished.

All that makes it imperative to redefine "general and complete" disarmament to make it compatible with the fragmented world that we envisage as persisting for the next half-century—a world of nation-states, autonomous centers of political and strategic initiative, occupied with their own self-defense, commanding some elements of force, and not reliant on a safety net in the form of an authoritative and potent world organization with effective police powers or, we might add, in the form of the ministrations of big alliance partners. It will also, no doubt, be a world still characterized by competitive nationalism and a measure of strategic distrust.

In these probable circumstances, disarmament should be pursued down to forces that cannot feasibly conduct aggressive war against other nations, but that will allow nations to conduct the defense of their citizens and their property against external attack. These forces—which would be conventional military forces—would be somewhat higher than the residual level envisaged in the U.S.-Soviet drafts of 1961-62. And the provisions of a disarmament program would also have to allow for some uneven implementation by the parties, a lack of meticulous reciprocity on some points, and some failures of detailed verification.

So "general and complete disarmament" will fall short of the ultimate and pure vision of two decades ago; though it will be much more sweeping than the "arms control" mechanisms we have relied on since then. But disarmament exercises should

---

In these probable circumstances, disarmament should be pursued down to forces that cannot feasibly conduct aggressive war against other nations, but that will allow nations to conduct the defense of their citizens and their property against external attack.

---

not be occasions for peace organizations to outbid each other in asserting perfect worlds and sweeping international regimes, fielding ingenious gimmicks, and displaying eloquent draftsmanship. The point is to introduce ends that are sustainable, a sequence that makes sense, a process that leads to more but can be stopped at any point with mutual profit and general stability. Thus disarmament could command the practical respect and the real allegiance of elites as well as bodies of citizens.

4. An Alternative Foreign Policy

Disarmament, however substantial, is not its own end. Disarmament must be shaped by, and be part of, a larger vision. In this proposal, the concepts that both inspire and encompass disarmament are (1) a different structure of international security and (2) a different kind of foreign policy.

For thirty years the United States has operated under the sway of a general paradigm that can be described in two key terms: *deterrence* (mostly at the level of strategic nuclear arms, including nuclear "umbrellas" and threats of the first use of nuclear weapons), and *alliance* (including deployments, bases, commitments, military assistance, proxy regimes, client states, the exportation of repressive technology, and an interest in political "stability")—quite a different objective from the benign condition of strategic stability.

These two elements, deterrence and alliance,

are mingled in different proportions in any concrete strategy toward a country or a region. When crosscut by constraints of budgetary pressures and public opinion that arise particularly in the wake of expensive, prolonged, and not notably successful military exercises, these elements emerge in rather different national strategies—as different as the "massive retaliation" and "New Look" of the Eisenhower-Dulles administration in the mid-1950s, and the "flexible response" of the Kennedy-McNamara administration in the early 1960s. Under the persistent paradigm of deterrence and alliance, there has been this comprehensible but barren alternation of defense postures and doctrines, each containing politically and technologically and strategically derived components, some of them self-contradictory and therefore subject to further shifts under the pressure of external challenges.

Unless the general paradigm of deterrence and alliance is fundamentally altered, we are condemned to periodic exercises of "brinkmanship"—credibility-enhancing regional confrontations, such as Cuba in 1962 and the Middle East in 1973; to periodic "limited wars," such as Korea and Vietnam; and to the hovering threat of global nuclear confrontation. It has been said that "deterrence works." It works, that is, until it fails. And then, because of the exaggerated retaliatory postures that have been adopted by both sides, "to strengthen deterrence," destruction is vastly aggravated. The cult of deterrence and the alliance system, therefore, should be replaced with a counter-paradigm of *war-avoidance* and *self-reliance*.

Such a fundamentally altered foreign policy need not proceed from the premise that the "other side" is up to nothing. It may be true that other nations are doing certain things that can't easily be explained in entirely benign ways. If we admit the probability of some troublesome behavior by others, and *still* want to obtain the benefits that would come from a revised security system, we may have to ask some more basic questions. They will be "so-what" questions, "can-we-live-with-that" questions. In answering them, we will have to overturn some notions that have been considered almost self-evident—such as the value of a military balance; not whether we are currently enjoying such a balance, but whether we need a military balance at all (as opposed to the more limited notion of stability, which is quite essential). Insistence on a proven and detailed military balance will impede progress toward reduction of arms and the risk of general war. Finite strategic sufficiency, at each stage of disarmament, is a valid and respectable condition; but balance is an elusive and capricious concept, and the quest for balance is more likely to amount to unending competition and, paradoxically, to perpetual instability.

A counter-paradigm of war-avoidance and self-

Insistence on a proven and detailed military balance will impede progress toward reduction of arms and the risk of general war.

reliance would devolve substantial defensive responsibilities upon our present allies. The effect would be to decouple the American strategic deterrent (and we might hope the strategic "umbrellas" of other nuclear guarantor countries) from the defense of regions.

In the short run, war-avoidance and self-reliance could lead to the revival of cooperative regional initiatives across the present East-West political boundaries (as we can hope and should plan). Conversely, they might lead to an uneven and in some cases competitive scramble by individual nations to compensate for the loss of immediate defensive resources and assurances. This is not easy to predict; but any of a number of possible outcomes is still preferable to the effects of the present situation of arms expansion and regional confrontations.

This position of non-intervention has been carelessly and gratuitously labeled "isolationism." It is not, and should be seen as an interim stage in an overall progression toward a comprehensive, at least semi-cooperative regime of international disarmament. A move by the large nuclear alliance guarantors to disengage from their tense and destructive commitments would be a most important impulse to the creation of a new security system.

5. Objectives

People in all countries are demanding the objectives of disarmament, even if they don't know precisely how to achieve them, even if their own leaders, who pretend to interpret these matters for them, see these objectives quite differently. The objectives of disarmament can be summarized in the word "security," in its principal senses of safety and social soundness. Reductions of the burdens of war preparation and reductions in the propensity to go to war, and restrictions of the destructive effects of war, would contribute directly to safety, and also to welfare and thereby indirectly to civil security.

These objectives translate into a more detailed and explicit list:
1. The prevention of war (greater stability of peace, fewer incentives to start a war);
2. In a conflict or confrontation, fewer incentives to escalate to the use of nuclear weapons;
3. In a conflict or an escalating confrontation, greater chance of re-establishing peace or lowering the level of conflict;

4. In a war, limitation of destruction, including, as an explicit objective, sparing civilians and innocent third parties, to the greatest extent possible;

5. In peacetime, lower costs of "defense" preparations, in money, conscription, and other social, environmental, psychological, and even moral aspects.

These objectives may conflict with each other. Some steps to reduce the chance of our own involvement in a war and therefore reduce the escalation of a war in its level and scope might, by lessening our own influence on diplomacy and crisis bargaining, make the incidence of war—somewhere, between other parties—more probable. Steps to reduce destruction to civilian populations might, by making the prospect of retaliation less terrible, make deterrence less effective and the strategic balance less stable. We have to pay some attention to these partially conflicting objectives; a balance must be sought between stability and contingent destruction, a balance that produces the lowest "expected damage." This formulation might sound somewhat arid, but the issues are not at all abstract; they have the most profound moral implications and strategic consequences.

Some of the concrete measures that we favor (not all of which are discussed in detail in this study) are:

● **In the area of strategic nuclear arms** (pending an across-the-board reduction and eventual abolition of all nuclear weapons):

Adoption of a doctrine of no first use of nuclear weapons;

Development of a very restricted targeting doctrine, refraining from aiming at civilians or concentrations of population that are closely collocated with military installations, and also avoiding the targeting of an adversary's missiles;

Announcement of a moratorium on the introduction of destabilizing new weapons systems, such as the MX intercontinental land-based missile, or long-range ground-launched or sea-launched cruise missiles (marginal improvements of present capabilities with no arguably undesirable effects on stability or lethality, such as the medium-range air-launched cruise missile or the Trident I submarine-launched missile, might be allowed to proceed);

An end to testing of all nuclear warheads in any environment, including underground (a "comprehensive test ban");

Stringent limitation on flight testing of new missiles;

Independent phasing out of increasingly vulnerable land-based missiles.

● **For nuclear weapons in general:**

Multilateral efforts to establish geographical zones that are nuclear-weapon-free.

● **With reference to nuclear materials and technology:**

Independent and multilateral efforts to curtail the proliferation of plutonium-based nuclear reactors;

Control of nuclear materials, both in use and wastes;

A halt, unilateral if necessary, in the production of fissionable materials for weapons.

● **In the area of other weapons of mass destruction:**

Outlawing of chemical and biological weapons.

● **Concerning conventional forces and weapons:**

Severe limitation on conventional arms transfers, including instruments of repression, with emphasis on preventing involvement by the producing nation in the strategic or political aims of the recipient.

● **In the area of general military dispositions and relationships** (the moves to be made reciprocally if possible, but independently if necessary):

Elimination of foreign military bases and troop deployments in foreign countries;

The ending, or in some cases transformation, of

The objectives of disarmament can be summarized in the word "security," in its principal senses of safety and social soundness.

---

military alliances;

Substantial cuts in military budgets, not just marginal reductions—for example, for the United States, on the order of twenty-five to forty percent as forces are reduced over a five- to ten-year period.

● **With regard to institutions and laws:**

Supranational mechanisms for peacekeeping, interposition, and mediation;

Confidence-building measures, such as inspectors, notification procedures, observers, hot lines;

Strengthening of the international rules of war;

Legal codes, within each country, to define criminal actions and fix accountability of official persons.

● **With reference to general and complete disarmament:**

A program of phased reductions, over all categories of arms and military infrastructure, with verification procedures.

Most of these explicit proposals have been seen before. Analyses, discussions, appeals, polemics, plans, blueprints, and schemes of disarmament compose a grand heap of material. There are over 9,000 listings in a current bibliography on this subject. Citations of urgency are becoming tedious.

But this time, the wolf might be at the gate of the stockade. It is not just a matter of the cumulation of weapons of vast lethality, or the continuing momentum of the arms race, or the monumental diversion of resources. That would be bad enough. Now a new element of precariousness and instability is being infused into the strategic balance. Virtually irreversible weapons initiatives are currently under active consideration in Congress and the Executive Branch.

At this moment, patronization and anodyne expressions will not do. Nor are conceptual neatness and legal perfection the point. We need some concrete moves of substantial disarmament. And we need to begin now.

Part Two: Some Proposals

6. The Quest for Strategic Stability

As we range over the disarmament initiatives proposed above, it is clear that many of these moves can be made independently, by the United States alone, even if it would be preferable if we could achieve reciprocity from other significant powers such as the Soviet Union.

One area where the United States could begin to reduce its forces independently, and in the process enhance its own security and the stability of the strategic balance, is the phasing out of our intercontinental ballistic missiles. The reasoning that underlies this judgment has to do with the logic of incentives.

Despite almost universal concentration on numbers—warheads, delivery vehicles, throw weight, megatons, equivalent megatons—numbers can't kill until they are used in war. Therefore, people ought to be interested in the stability of the strategic balance. The strategic balance consists of the pattern of incentives, for both sides, to initiate or not to initiate nuclear war under a variety of circumstances. Further, the circumstances that ought to be of most interest are not the placid moments in international relations, but the crisis situations—those rare and rather improbable situations that are, nonetheless, reckonable and at the foundation of the arms race and the bellicose postures of the powers of the world.

The technical factors that go into the strategic balance—the types of weapons, their location, their peculiar characteristics and effects—shape the logic of incentives. When we do our homework on these technical factors, we find that we must take seriously the contention of the hawks that certain portions of our nuclear forces will become vulnerable to a first strike by the forces of the Soviet Union, by the early to mid-1980s. (In turn, the land-based forces of the Soviet Union are becoming vulnerable to a counterforce strike by the United States.) However improbable such a strike might be, even under the most extreme circumstances of a confrontation, this is the measure of nuclear stability, and it is the fact that is driving the next stage of the arms race.

The vulnerability of our land-based missiles has led to the development of the next generation of nuclear weapons systems, particularly the MX missile, the replacement for our present Minutemen. And considerations of stability give rise to fears about moves already being executed to "improve" the capabilities of the Minutemen; the potent MK-12A warheads (350 kilotons) and the accurate NS-20 guidance system (within one-tenth of a nautical mile). These two improvements, fitted onto the present 550 Minuteman III missiles, could threaten Soviet missiles in their silos, thereby needling the Russians in a crisis to launch their missiles preemptively. Such a decision would be reinforced by the fact that our improved Minutemen would still be stationary targets for the Russians; in short, our land-based missile force would have the worst—the most unstable—combination of characteristics.

The Carter administration has recognized the emerging technical "threat" to our present fixed land-based missiles. That is one reason why it proposed, at Moscow in March 1977, "deep cuts," particularly cuts in Soviet "heavy missiles," that would neutralize the Russians' capacity to strike at our nuclear forces. In short, the Carter administration was—and is—looking to the SALT process (the formal strategic arms limitation talks) for a solution to our looming strategic problems. The trouble is that the SALT process—particularly the current round, SALT II—is unlikely to produce an agreement sufficient to eradicate the technical threat to our land-based missiles and thus to cure the growing instability of the strategic balance.

That is not a reason to denigrate or to oppose SALT. We should support the process as, perhaps, a "necessary" element in a comprehensive commitment to arms reduction. But we must look beyond SALT. We must backstop SALT by making independent national moves.

In this developing situation, the two most important moves we could make—and they are moves we can make independently—would be, not a simple reduction in numbers, but: (1) elimination of our own provocative counterforce capability, in the MK-12A warhead and the NS-20 guidance system that we are already introducing into our Minuteman force; and (2) elimination of the technical vulnerability of our land-based missiles to Soviet attack.

Some propose that the latter purpose could be achieved by making our land-based missiles mobile—that is, moving to the MX. And indeed, mobility is the least objectionable feature of the proposed MX system (except for the fact that mobility, or multiple basing, would confuse the effort to verify numbers of missiles, and so possibly complicate future arms control agreements). The arguments against "going mobile" with the MX are its extreme cost (estimated at close to $50 billion to deploy about 300 missiles); its provocative and destabilizing effects because of its high MIRV-carrying capacity (up to 14 warheads), the relatively high yield of each warhead (about 200 kilotons), and their projected accuracy (within 100 yards); the fact that the MX, even in its mobile or multiple basing mode, would still be vulnerable to a high expenditure of Soviet warheads against it; and, not least, the fact that it is not necessary—there is an obvious alternative, the complete elimination of our land-based missile force, over the next five or ten years, as it becomes vulnerable to improvements in the Soviet

---

These independent moves would not be mere bargaining ploys, just so much psychological bait, to be cancelled or reversed if not reciprocated. They make strategic sense in themselves, and therefore can be sustained, whether or not they are reciprocated.

---

missile force. The latter is the recommendation of this study.

We would move, thereby, from the present triad of strategic nuclear systems to a diad, consisting of submarine-based ballistic missiles, and stand-off bombers equipped with medium-range air-launched cruise missiles. That would be a force that would serve the United States sufficiently for deterrent purposes, during the first phase of a more general arms reduction sequence.

Our sea-based missiles would have to be sufficiently accurate—and no more than that—and low in yield to accomplish a more restricted and more precise mission, distinguishing purely military targets (but not the strictly counterforce targets of Soviet missile silos). In an intermediate range of time—though not on the present accelerated schedule—we would deploy the longer-range Trident I (or C-4)

missile in our present Poseidon submarines, allowing them to operate farther from their targets, closer to their bases, and in more area of ocean, further enhancing their invulnerability by complicating an enemy's anti-submarine warfare.

These independent moves would not be mere bargaining ploys, just so much psychological bait, to be cancelled or reversed if not reciprocated. They make strategic sense in themselves, and therefore can be sustained, whether or not they are reciprocated.

Though strategic stability, not cost, is the primary motive for making independent moves, cost savings would not be negligible. Moving to a diad of submarines and manned bombers, instead of the present triad, would eventually reduce the annual cost of our strategic nuclear forces from $25 billion to $18 billion (in 1979 dollars).

But the principal justification for these changes in our nuclear posture remains their contribution to enhancing strategic stability, to eliminating an enemy's incentive under virtually any circumstances to escalate to the first use of nuclear weapons to strike our nuclear forces (it would make no sense for any nation to initiate an escalation to nuclear war by attacking the other side's cities rather than its nuclear forces). In a more general sense, taking certain independent initatives to make our own nuclear forces invulnerable helps to begin a more comprehensive program of disarmament, by *disconnecting* our security from "the Soviet threat."

7. No First Use of Nuclear Weapons

Nuclear war can occur only if someone starts it—that is, if a nation strikes first with nuclear weapons. Therefore, perhaps the most important move toward a less dangerous world is for nations to adopt, and to build into their defensive plans and postures, an intention not to use nuclear weapons first.

The international legal mechanics of no first use—though these are often stressed—are less important than embodying the intention and expectation of no first use in the tangible weapons systems and actual doctrines of nations. It is also less important to achieve unanimity, or even bilateral reciprocity, in a pledge of no first use, or formal acceptance of the principle in a binding treaty, than it is to start independently and expand the adoption by individual nations of the principle and the stance of no first use. We should try to negotiate such an agreement among nations, particularly between the United States and the Soviet Union; but we should not shrink from adopting no first use independently. Above all, we should not require reciprocity as a necessary condition for our moving to a no first use doctrine, and we should not dangle our possible adherence to such a doctrine as a bargaining chip for achieving other strategic objectives in formal negotiations.

We can and should move to a doctrine of no first use, even independently and unconditionally, because it would enhance our own security and further enhance the stability of the world strategic balance. Of course, there are some hypothetical circumstances—say, a failing conventional defense of Western Europe—in which our allies might lose territory or forfeit their political integrity if we were to abandon the option, or the threat, of resorting to the first use of nuclear weapons, tactical or strategic. Indeed, that scenario is the principal source of objections, within the United States and Europe, to the adoption of a no first use doctrine, and the principal source of the notion that we need to continue our "extended deterrence"—which is actually the threat of our first use of nuclear weapons. For this reason, some ostensible proposals of "no first use" would exempt the European theater from the application of this principle, pending a successful outcome of some other set of negotiations—say, Mutual and Balanced Force Reductions (MBFR). But, since Europe is the most likely case, and the most important case, for the use of nuclear weapons, such an exception doesn't do much to establish the rule.

In this respect, we should be clear about President Carter's address to the United Nations on October 4, 1977, in which some of his rhetoric raised hopes and inspired tenuous interpretations that he was putting forward the equivalent of a no first use doctrine. True, he said that the United States "will not use nuclear weapons except in self-defense"; but he went on to define self-defense as "circumstances of an actual nuclear *or conventional* attack on the United States, our territories or armed forces, *or such an attack on allies."* This is no change from our traditional doctrine. In other words, we are still relying on a nuclear response to redeem a losing conventional battle, particularly in central Europe. Our present policy is a prescription for converting regional defense into global holocaust.

A policy of no first use of nuclear weapons has both strategic and moral foundations. The strategic and the moral considerations are intertwined. An amplification of the moral considerations involved in nuclear doctrine might be in order at this point.

A nuclear strategy designed to meet stringent moral requisites would have two main concerns: First, it would, as far as possible, avoid civilian deaths if ever there were an occasion to join in a nuclear war, even in response to another nation's attack on our own homeland. That would imply strict limitations on the targeting of our nuclear forces. (We will treat the subject of targeting in a later section.)

The second moral requisite—more to the point in this discussion of no first use of nuclear weapons—would be to minimize the possibility of ever using nuclear weapons in the first place. This would have two components. The first is to reduce the chance that we would ever provoke or tempt an adversary to

We can and should move to a doctrine of no first use, even independently and unconditionally, because it would enhance our own security and further enhance the stability of the world strategic balance.

wage a first strike against our nuclear forces and thus precipitate our second strike. This, in turn, implies reducing the incentive for such a strike against us by removing the vulnerability of our own force, and also reducing the potential disarming, or first-strike, propensity that might be built into our force. (These moves were discussed in the preceding section.)

But a second component is necessary. We must put a double lock on nuclear war by foreclosing the possibility that we ourselves might escalate to the first use of nuclear weapons. In past years, a first strike by us was technologically improbable, since our missiles did not have the accuracy (coupled with yield) to destroy reliably a sufficient portion of an adversary's nuclear force to "limit damage" to ourselves from his retaliatory strike. Our land-based missiles have acquired this capability. But now, even if we were to give up our land-based missiles, we would still not avoid the temptation, in a severe crisis, to strike first, since accurate guidance will soon be available for our sea-based missiles as well.

Thus, to minimize the possibility of ever using nuclear weapons, we must impose upon ourselves a stringent doctrine of no first use of nuclear weapons. We should encourage others to join us in such a policy (the Soviets have long favored a no first use pledge); but it would make sense to impose this restraint upon ourselves, whether or not we get formal reciprocity. No first use is not an idle demonstration of "good intentions," to impress the Russians or others, who might nonetheless remain unimpressed. The purpose is to impress ourselves—to remove our own incentive to escalate, to force ourselves to change the basis of our entire national strategy.

Our homeland, cities, population, property, political system, civil arrangements, social structures—everything we have—can be destroyed only if we invite an enemy's direct attack. We have every strategic, as well as moral, reason to adopt a no first use doctrine. And that is entirely separate from the more philosophical point that, if all nations were to adopt such a doctrine, as a kind of "categorical imperative," nuclear war would be impossible.

8. The Targeting of Weapons and the Protection of Non-Combatants

A disarmament program should seek not only to avoid war, but also to minimize and restrict destruction in war. Confining destruction in war—which amounts, practically, to the protection of innocent non-combatants—has rightly been considered a mark and a measure of the progress of civilization. But this principle has eroded in recent decades with the progressive increase in the destructive power of modern weapons. The advent of nuclear weapons, finally, constituted a change in the kind, not just the degree, of warfare and challenged the use or threat of war as a recourse for settling international disputes, achieving national ambitions, or even attaining justice for disadvantaged and repressed groups.

Perversely, nuclear weapons have also given birth to a contrary "logic," that has become generally accepted, even though it defies the development of civilized norms for the protection of non-combatants: Since nuclear weapons are capable of widespread annihiliation, and since they are difficult to use in a relatively discriminating way, a certain doctrine for their employment, massive counter-city retaliation, has become equated with the very notion of deterrence and nuclear stability, and has become the preferred formula of the arms controllers—the "doves"—for nuclear restraint. These facts have prompted even the most humane analysts and legislators to make a wide exception for the deliberate use, or the calculated threat, of nuclear weapons, in a mode of unlimited destruction.* Indeed, so far have we retrogressed in our conception of the morality of warfare—influenced by the warped logic of nuclear strategy—that we consider civil defense to constitute an ominous signal of aggressive intent.

The dovish position on targeting, leaning heavily on the deliberate threat to civilian populations, is no improvement on the "massive retaliation" formula of John Foster Dulles, in the 1950s. Until recently, measures to reduce the likelihood of nuclear war (the other profound moral principle that should govern our defensive measures and our moves to disarmament) have consisted primarily of increasing the contingent probability and horror of retaliation against civilians (i.e., countervalue).

---

*Thus, even such an acute and sympathetic commentator as Professor Thomas J. Farer, in his presentation to the U.S. House of Representatives Subcommittee on Courts, Civil Liberties, and the Administration of Justice, on H.R. 8388, the "Official Accountability Act," on February 2, 1976, makes an exception, in his otherwise comprehensive prohibition of retaliation against population centers, to condone the indiscriminate threat or use of nuclear weapons (pp. 42 ff).

This effect has been reinforced by the fact that the weapons systems expected to survive a preemptive attack—air-delivered and submarine-launched bombs and missiles—have also been those that, because of their inaccuracy, have been relatively restricted to civilian targets. Some reluctant dovish advocates of countervalue targeting, who want its stability without its immorality, say that it is permissible to threaten to do something that one might not actually have to do. But this is a cop-out: They have no right to assume perfect deterrence in order to absolve themselves of serious moral choice. Moreover, if you base your entire policy on a certain threat, preparing to do certain things and failing to prepare to do alternative things, then you are disposing yourself to execute the moves you threaten.

These intimations of destruction are so momentous that we cannot evade the question of targeting in any proposal of disarmament. Even if the measures of disarmament presented here were adopted, the possibility of war could not be absolutely ruled out. And during a phased sequence of disarmament, as long as some nuclear weapons are retained, they will implicitly be aimed at something.

Having said that, however, as a kind of admonition to the peacemakers, we should also make something clear to the "realists." There are only four possible answers to the question of targeting, even if we assume a strict second-strike doctrine and assume that our homeland has been struck first with nuclear weapons:

(1) Plan to limit further damage by striking an adversary's remaining missiles in their silos. But that doctrine and the accompanying posture would encourage adversaries to plan to launch on warning, frustrating our damage-limiting intent and magnifying the danger to our population.

(2) Strike the adversary's cities, in a massive, countervalue retaliatory attack. But, even if an adversary's attack had destroyed our cities, in this almost unimaginable situation *nothing* would seem "worth" doing. It is just as conceivable—and properly so—that a president, or his survivor, would not push the button as that he would. The point is that striking "enemy" populations, *even then,* would make no more strategic sense than it ever did, and no moral sense at all.

(3) Do nothing. This targeting option, which is actually the limiting case, a non-targeting option, is of course scarcely within the horizon of discussable alternatives. But what is so irrational about it, if we care about human life and not just revenge? This position should be aired and accorded respect, even though it is outside the present range of "responsible" thinking on nuclear strategies. Positing this limiting option at least has the effect of putting all the other options in a sharper perspective and shifting the center of gravity from the first two responses, which are now conceived as "moderate"

(retaliation against cities, and counterforce in the strict sense of planning to strike the enemy's unexpended nuclear forces), toward the other end of the range of alternative targeting doctrines.

(4) Specifically, our consideration should be shifted to a fourth targeting doctrine which repre-

> **Even with an extremely limited target list, however, we have to realize that the entire area of the use of nuclear weapons, because of their characteristic nature and their probable collateral effects, is fraught with the danger of crime.**

sents the most severe limitation that has yet been practically proposed: (a) Completely avoid hitting cities. (b) Specifically avoid counterforce in its strict sense of targeting the adversary's time-sensitive nuclear forces, such as land-based missiles, which would then be more likely to be launched on warning or even preemptively. (c) Aim our nuclear forces (at whatever stage of nuclear disarmament we had achieved) at strictly military, military-industrial, and logistical targets. And further, (d) avoid even those military targets if they are closely collocated with population centers. (That, and that alone, would be the rationale for allowing the development of accuracy on our nuclear weapons; and even then, already planned accuracies are sufficient to accomplish this degree of discrimination.)

It could be objected that a restriction of targeting would dilute the fear of retaliation upon which deterrence rests and consequently unhinge the stability of the strategic balance. This is not only a strategic problem, but, at one remove, a moral one, as would be any proposal that might increase the incidence of nuclear war. The first rejoinder is that it should be possible, observing stringent criteria of sparing noncombatants, to construct a plausible list of targets that would be sufficient for deterrence, without spilling over into the areas of nuclear provocation or mass destruction—in short, avoiding both counterforce and countervalue. Indeed, some would argue that any enemy who is willing to initiate nuclear war might care more about having his military forces defeated and the sinews of his political control strained and conceivably snapped than he might care about protecting his civilian population. The second rejoinder (as we suggested above, in introducing the moral framework for the consideration of nuclear weapons) is that the probability of war and the contingent infliction and suffering of casualties in war must be considered, not in isolation, but together, in a calculation of "expected damage." In such a calculation, we believe that restricted targeting is preferable to brandishing the threat of indiscriminate mass destruction.

Even with an extremely limited target list, however, we have to realize that the entire area of the use of nuclear weapons, because of their characteristic nature and their probable collateral effects, is fraught with the danger of crime. In fact, nuclear targeting is only a case—though a leading case—of a more general proscription against involving civilians in the consequences of war. With regard to this larger protection of civilians, we should advance and reinforce work that is in process among nations. A cardinal opportunity to strengthen the contemporary foundation of civilian protection presents itself in the two "Protocols Additional to the Geneva Conventions of 12 August 1949, and Relating to the Protection of Victims of International Armed Conflict." Presented in July 1977 to the Geneva Conference on Humanitarian Law (attended by the United States and 120 other nations), the protocols were adopted in December 1977 and are open for signature. The provisions of these protocols are not vague or impractical; they are constructive and clearly drafted. They should be supported within the executive branch; hearings should be conducted by the Senate Foreign Relations Committee; and a wider audience should be provided among groups of citizens.

Some of the provisions have a close bearing on the use of nuclear weapons. It is hard to see how the humane and discriminating intentions of these protocols could be implemented with the postures, weapons systems, and doctrines that are now embodied in our nuclear strategies. Even the section that applies to combatants (Part III, pp. 25 ff.) specifies (Article 35, paragraph 2) that "it is prohibited to employ weapons, projectiles and materials and methods of warfare of a nature to cause superfluous injury or unnecesary suffering"; and (Article 35, paragraph 3) that "it is prohibited to employ methods or means of warfare which are intended, or may be expected, to cause widespread, long-term and severe damage to the natural environment." And Article 36 of that section, on "New Weapons," specifies:

In the study, development, acquisition or adoption of a new weapon, means or method of warfare, a High Contracting Party is under an obligation to determine whether its employment would, in some or all circumstances, be prohibited by this Protocol or by any other rule of international law applicable to the High Contracting Party.

Part IV, on "Civilian Population," Section I, "General Protection Against Effects of Hostilities," contains the provisions that are most restrictive of the use of nuclear weapons. Chapter I, "Basic Rules and Field of Application," states (Article 48):

. . . the Parties to the conflict shall at all times distinguish between the civilian population and combatants and between civilian objects and military objectives and accordingly shall direct their operations only against military ob-

jectives.

This provision alone would seem to rule out our present strategy—now traditional after the better part of two decades of adherence—of holding civilian populations hostage and deliberately planning massive retaliatory attacks against cities. Again, this section of the protocol states (Article 51, paragraph 2):

The civilian population as such, as well as individual civilians, shall not be the object of attack. Acts or threats of violence the primary purpose of which is to spread terror among the civilian population are prohibited.

And a still later paragraph (6) reinforces this intent to deny the doctrine of massive counter-city retaliation: "Attacks against the civilian population or civilians by way of reprisals are prohibited."

Other passages seem to rule out attacks even on military objectives that are near significantly populated areas (Article 51, paragraph 4): "Indiscriminate attacks are prohibited," and are defined as, among other things, "(a) those which are directed at a specific military objective"; and "(b) those which employ a method or means of combat which cannot be directed at a specific military objective . . . and consequently, in each such case, are of a nature to strike military objectives and civilians or civilian objects without distinction." Also proscribed in this section are (paragraph 5):

(a) an attack by bombardment by any methods or means which treats as a single military objective a number of clearly separated and distinct military objectives located in a city, town, village or other area containing a similar concentration of civilians or civilian objects; and (b) an attack which may be expected to cause incidental loss of civilian life, injury to civilians, damage to civilian objects, or a combination thereof, which would be excessive in relation to the concrete and direct military advantage anticipated.

The list of proscribed objects is broadened to include (Article 54, paragraph 2): "objects indispensable to the survival of the civilian population, such as foodstuffs, agricultural areas for the production of foodstuffs, crops, livestock, drinking water installations and supplies and irrigation works." Also (Article 55, paragraph 1): "Care shall be taken in warfare to protect the natural environment against widespread, long-term and severe damage." Dams and dikes are also to be protected (Article 56, paragraph 1).

One provision suggests the criteria by which a target list must be constructed (Chapter IV, "Precautionary Measures," Article 57, "Precautions in Attack," paragraph 3):

When a choice is possible between several military objectives for obtaining a similar military advantage, the objective to be selected shall be that the attack on which may be expected to cause the least danger to civilian lives and to civilian objects.

Further sections of the protocols contain suggestions of locating legal responsibility for repression of breaches of the protective ordinances (Section II, "Repression of Breaches of the Conventions and of This Protocol," especially Articles 86 and 87), including the admonition (Article 86, paragraph 2) that "the fact that a breach of the Conventions or of this Protocol was committed by a subordinate does not absolve his superiors from penal or disciplinary responsibility." These are suggestions, not only of the location of responsibility, but the possibility of criminal prosecution. We consider this line of development to be of the highest importance to the cause of arms restrictions, and we expand on this in a later section of this paper.

The point of these citations is not merely to promote the adoption of these particular protocols—though they are important—by the United States and other nations, but to indicate the direction in which the restriction of acts of mass destruction in war should go. These kinds of provisions, coupled with the definition of criminal activity and the ascription of individual responsibility, would, if incorporated into our domestic law, constitute the basic legal framework for regulating the conduct of our leaders and the actions of our country in waging or even threatening to wage war. People in all countries should move for the adoption of these protocols, not only for their particular restrictive provisions, but for the education they would afford, to leaders, civilian and military, as well as citizens, and for the improvement of the international moral climate that surrounds the prospective use of weapons, particularly strategic nuclear weapons.

9. The Problem of Tactical Nuclear Weapons

Tactical nuclear weapons are employed within a "theater," such as Western Europe, and generally on or relatively close behind the battlefield. They can be distinguished from strategic nuclear weapons, which are defined as capable of hitting the homelands of the United States and the Soviet Union (though this distinction, particularly in a European conflict, is often blurred). Tactical nuclear weapons consist of a variety of dimensions and yields of warheads, types of delivery systems, and locations.

These weapons present a special problem in the prevention of war, and also in the minimizing of destruction in war, since (1) although ostensibly designed only for attack on military objectives, they provide a bridge—an avenue for escalation—between conventional warfare and the use of intercontinental strategic nuclear weapons and thus open up the possibility of a global conflict; and (2) they promise an extreme intensification of destruction even within the theater, to combatants and civilians too, and thus raise the questions that never before had to be contemplated in the immediate battlefield environment.

Many of these aspects of tactical nuclear weapons are present in the debate about the introduction of the "neutron bomb" into the U.S. arsenal in Europe. The neutron bomb (or more properly the neutron, or enhanced radiation, weapon) is actually a nuclear artillery shell (for the 8-inch and 155-mm howitzer, maximum range 20 miles) and a missile warhead (for the LANCE missile, range 56 miles). It relies on enhanced radiation, rather than blast or heat, to accomplish its lethal effect. Detonated at rather high altitudes above its target, it has comparatively little radioactive fallout. Thus its lethal effects are said to be more controllable, more "discrete," and its "collateral damage" to non-combatants and civilian structures is sharply reduced. In addition, since its radiation would be massive but short-lived, enemy-held areas that were attacked with the neutron weapon, rather than with "ordinary" tactical nuclear weapons, would be available sooner for reoccupation.

We should grasp the larger problem of tactical nuclear weapons, and consider the complete elimination of this category of weapons from all theaters...

Ironically, the asserted "advantages" of the neutron weapon are those that cause the alarm: (1) the limited collateral destruction to nearby civilian populations—supposedly friendly populations, since, by the time the authorization for its use has been given, a battle would presumably be in process on the soil of our allies; (2) the unique means of reaching inside protected tanks and armored personnel vehicles; and (3) the sparing of structures. For the danger with this weapon is not that it won't do what it is supposed to do; rather, that it might do it too well (though even its specific performance features have come under challenge). Of course, the neutron weapon was designed precisely for the greater feasibility of its use. But the effects are mixed: Supposedly greater feasibility of use makes it a more credible deterrent to the initiation by the other side of tactical nuclear war—or indeed of conventional war. But, to the contrary, if we were already in a conventional war, our own initial use of these nuclear weapons would be more probable; thus, the greater usability of this weapon is its principal defect.

For these specific reasons, and because of its other liabilities, further development and deployment of the neutron weapon should be cancelled. (Retaining it as a bargaining chip, as President Carter decided to do in April, 1978, might get the worst of both worlds.) But the neutron weapon is just an example of the larger problem. It is typical of the kind of "improvement" of tactical nuclear weapons that will be constantly sought, as long as this category of arms is relied on to fill a certain "gap" in the spectrum of warfare and deterrence. Not only should this particular weapon be cancelled, but we should grasp the larger problem of tactical nuclear weapons, and consider the complete elimination of this category of weapons from all theaters, including Europe, and ultimately from our stockpiles, as part of a more general phased program of disarmament.

Of course, as in the case of the elimination or attenuation of other weapons and types of forces, it can be asserted that regional "security," specifically the security of our allies, will suffer. That is part of a much larger phase of the general debate about alliance policy and a substantially disarmed world. But surely the loss of this specific element of deterrence is more than compensated by the reduced danger of escalation of a regional conflict to global proportions.

10. The Testing of Weapons

A Comprehensive Nuclear Test Ban

The arguments for a comprehensive nuclear test ban have been aired for two decades and are well enough known not to required detailed treatment here. A complete halt of the testing of nuclear explosives—in all environments (in the atmosphere, in outer space, under water, and underground), and including all types of explosions (weapons and "peaceful nuclear explosions" or PNEs), and affecting all sizes of explosion—would be a most effective way of braking the qualitative aspects of the arms race and discouraging nuclear proliferation.

Nuclear testing in the atmosphere, in outer space, and under water have already been banned by the 1963 Limited Test Ban Treaty. A comprehensive test ban was envisaged in that treaty itself, and in the Treaty on the Non-Proliferation of Nuclear Weapons of 1968.

Two further agreements relating to testing have been negotiated, beyond the Limited Test Ban Treaty of 1963: the 1974 Threshold Test Ban Treaty, prohibiting underground tests of weapons larger than 150 kilotons and contemplating verification by national means, seismic and satellite; and the 1976

Treaty on Underground Nuclear Explosions (the "PNE Treaty"), banning peaceful underground explosions larger than 150 kilotons, with verification by national means and the presence of observers from the other nation at the site of certain large, multiple tests.

Both of these treaties were submitted to the Senate in 1976, but have not yet been ratified. The problems are the high limit of 150 kilotons (cf. the Hiroshima bomb yield of 15-20 kilotons), and the fact that the PNE Treaty legitimizes peaceful nuclear explosions, which cannot be distinguished from weapons tests. There are dangers both in ratification and in non-ratification. The danger of ratification is that it would "take the heat off" a comprehensive test ban. The contrasting danger of decisive rejection by the Senate is that the whole issue of test bans would be sent back to the drawing board, progress in negotiations would be discouraged, and wrong signals would be given of American intentions.

In a resolution on March 24, 1977, the Senate proposed that the United States and the Soviet Union observe a moratorium on all underground nuclear explosions and begin negotiations for a permanent treaty to ban all nuclear explosions. And in June 1977 negotiations toward a comprehensive test ban were renewed between the United States (with the U.K.) and the Soviet Union at Geneva. These negotiations should be supported.

The partial treaties can be received positively, but only with the understanding that they are way-stations, in some respects useful (for example, the exchange of other-country observers confirms the principle of on-site inspection—even though technical progress in seismic detection, down to about one kiloton, is said to have virtually eliminated the need for on-site inspection to prevent significant cheating that could affect the security of a signatory state). Furthermore, every effort should be made to involve China and France, and any other nuclear or threshold nuclear nation, in such a comprehensive treaty. But such involvement need not preclude an agreement between the two superpowers (and the U.K.), with their large qualitative and quantitative lead in nuclear weaponry.

Flight Testing

An associated move would be a stringent limitation on flight testing of improved missiles, designed to perfect the technology of MIRV (multiple independently-targetable re-entry vehicles) and accuracy. Such a limitation on flight tests—no more than six tests of intercontinental range a year—was suggested in President Carter's "Moscow comprehensive" proposal in March 1977. But this proposal was rejected by the Soviets, and testing is unlikely to be limited through bilateral negotiations to a frequency low enough completely to halt qualitative advances in MIRVing and accuracy. (Thus, the argument for independent moves by the United States to take fixed land-based weapons out of the area of vulnerability remains valid.)

Since the United States has a large lead in the kinds of technology that require flight testing, we should take the initative and declare an independent moratorium on these tests. Bilateral progress might or might not ensue, but we would lose little, if anything, in the effort.

11. Geographical Restrictions

Nuclear-Weapon-Free Zones

An approach to disarmament that complements the other moves and attacks the problem in another dimension is the establishment of geographical limitations. "Nuclear-weapon-free zones" (NWFZs) envisage the complete prohibition of nuclear weapons in the defined area, and the agreement of outside nuclear powers not to introduce or threaten to introduce nuclear weapons into the area. Such a zone has been established in Latin America through the Treaty of Tlatelolco in 1967 (though this agreement has not yet been ratified by Argentina, and Brazil has taken some exceptions relating to peaceful use).

Similar regional proposals for nuclear-weapon-free zones have been made for Scandinavia, the Balkans, the Mediterranean, Africa, South Asia, and the South Pacific. Though somewhat confused and either fragmentary or overlapping, such proposals should be supported. The object, and the criterion, of these moves, as others in the inventory of disarmament, are not neatness or legal meticulousness. They are coverage, momentum, direction, commitment. To date, such proposals have merely nibbled away at the fringes of the most significant areas of

---

Since the United States has a large lead in the kinds of technology that require flight testing, we should take the initiative and declare an independent moratorium on these tests.

---

possible nuclear confrontation, the places where the largest regional stockpiles of theater weapons are located; they do not intrude on the center of these areas, particularly Central Europe. A proposal to eliminate nuclear weapons from Central Europe should be framed and advanced at this point, mostly to demonstrate that this critical area, too—perhaps especially—is in need of such a restriction.

Zones of Peace

The concept of the zone of peace is broader and

less specifically related to nuclear weapons. It refers to such arrangements as the one proposed by the littoral states of the Indian Ocean, in an attempt to exclude the deployment and maneuver of outside military forces, such as those of the United States and the Soviet Union. Such efforts should be encouraged and pursued by the regional states; and the larger outside powers should be pressed to join in negotiations, with each other and multilaterally with the regional states, to conform to such prohibitions.

We should adopt the attitude that wherever such arrangements for zones of peace, even partial, can be attained, they are worth achieving, even if the pattern is largely fortuitous and the sequence not particularly logical. We need the actions themselves, the progressive exclusion of great-power military maneuvering from areas of the world; but we also need the demonstrations of what is possible, encouraging regional states themselves to become interested in the possibilities of arms limitation in their areas.

12. Controls on Nuclear Proliferation

The problem of nuclear proliferation has two aspects: weapons, and "peaceful" uses of nuclear materials.

The Non-Proliferation Treaty of 1968, which now has 102 adherents, was an important step, and we should encourage the remaining non-signatories to join in this pact. But we can't afford to be too optimistic. Even signatory non-nuclear nations can develop weapons capabilities under the threshold of the treaty's restrictions. The treaty can be denounced on 90 days notice, for self-judged reasons of national security. Coercive measures to influence compliance of other countries would be either ineffective or counter-productive. Some of the most critical potential nuclear and almost-nuclear powers remain outside of the Non-Proliferation Treaty—having either failed to sign or failed to ratify (France, Israel, Brazil, Argentina, India, Pakistan, South Africa, and Egypt)—and there are pervasive incentives for many of these countries not to adhere to this regime.

The Carter administration has made strong efforts to postpone the widespread installation of the plutonium cycle. But these efforts, too, and those of non-governmental groups, cause us to realize how intractable this problem is likely to be.

We have to recognize nuclear proliferation, not as a technical problem in itself, but as an aspect of the emerging many-power world. Indeed, the tendency to the fragmentation of military power and

In view of the actual situation, the standard horatory arguments, to the effect that "we must not fail" to stop nuclear proliferation, are not less valid; they are simply obsolete. We have already failed. The question now is how to live in a partially proliferated world.

political initiative has been exacerbated by the decline of American reliability, both as an alliance guarantor and as a supplier of critical resources, in this case nuclear fuel. Further steps to curtail American political-military intrusion into the politics of other regions and the affairs of other states might, as a byproduct, contribute to the further fragmentation of power and initative, and thus in some ways to the probability of further nuclear proliferation. This will be true despite the countervailing exemplary effect of American self-restraint in the development and deployment of nuclear arms and the use of nuclear energy.

In other words, nuclear proliferation is both a cause and an effect of the tendency of the international system to general unalignment. One of the principal reasons why nuclear proliferation is such a stubborn problem is that it is built into the very evolution of the international system. That is why it is not particularly compelling, though it is depressing, to see a succession of lists of "nuclear powers" or "threshold nuclear powers" in Year X (according to one prediction, by the U.S. Department of Energy, at least 6 now, 15 within three years, 26 within six years, 35 within ten years). That is just the background of the problem and doesn't in itself suggest any particular solution. Moreover, every solution has its costs. To the extent that the restraint of "horizontal" proliferation is achieved at the cost of extending "nuclear umbrellas" and offering other alliance guarantees, it interferes with other aspects of the attempt to limit wars and stop the nuclear arms race, or "vertical proliferation." The cure can be as bad as the disease.

There are many reasons for nations to acquire nuclear forces of some kind and dimension, as well as peaceful nuclear technology for the production of energy. A principal reason is the widespread perception that the superpowers will not make good on their guarantees to smaller, non-nuclear allies in situations of challenge to those smaller allies. The increasing prudence of the two superpowers is already a factor in the tendency of lesser states to acquire nuclear capabilities. Nations that have made moves, or noises, for this reason include France, China, India, Israel, South Korea, and Iran, and may some day include Japan.

Other reasons for nuclear acquisition are the fear of neighbors (whether or not those neighbors have actually acquired nuclear weapons first); the quest for dominance in a region or sub-region; and the "exemplar" effect—the argument that others have them, that nuclear weapons are part of the trappings of sovereignty. In view of the actual situation, the standard horatory arguments, to the effect that "we must not fail" to stop nuclear proliferation, are not less valid; they are simply obsolete. We have already failed. The question now is how to live in a partially proliferated world.

Nevertheless, we must do what we can to slow or impede the process of nuclear diffusion, without impairing the transition to a war-free international system, or at least to a system in which the United States is not inevitably involved in every conflict, as a guarantor. For sooner or later we arrive at the question of sanctions. The crux of the matter of nonproliferation is enforcement. Unfortunately, most schemes of enforcement against states that detonate nuclear devices, divert fissionable materials to weapons production, or refuse to allow inspection of their nuclear facilities imply measures, up to and including the resort to armed force, that are hardly better than the abuse. Active and coercive measures, particularly the use of military force, whether by a supranational agency or by individual nations, should be discouraged. There must be reliance on lesser measures, even if they are much less

---

The temporary banning and early superseding of plutonium by denatured or alternative and safer fuels would seem to be the most urgent task in the control of nuclear proliferation.

---

active and rely on other means of influence. They might consist of exposure and condemnation, and range through suspension of diplomatic relations, interruption of communications, to the imposition of economic sanctions.

The methods of control might be collaborative or unilateral. We should favor the expansion of the activities and capabilities of the International Atomic Energy Agency, with regard to the safeguarding and monitoring of national nuclear facilities, and perhaps the worldwide inventorying of nuclear fuels. We should attempt to secure an international agreement by potential nuclear suppliers not to transfer facilities for enrichment of nuclear fuel or reprocessing of spent fuel from reactors. (The most likely forum for such measures is the "London Supplier Group," a group of fifteen nations, including the Soviet Union, which meet informally to coordinate their policies for exporting nuclear technology and equipment.) But here, perhaps, "the genie is out of the bottle," with the deals between France and Pakistan and between Germany and Brazil. Surplus capacity and sharp competition among producers of nuclear equipment may defeat future international efforts to curtail the proliferation of facilities capable of generating weapons-grade nuclear material. For the longer run, we should encourage research in nuclear fuel cycles that are less susceptible to the diversion of material for nuclear weapons than the plutonium cycle, yet more efficient than the present once-through uranium cycle. Even within the generally risky area of nuclear energy production, there is a vast difference between types of fuel cycle: roughly between those cycles that "burn" nuclear fuel and use enriched uranium (and also can use recycled plutonium), and those cycles that "breed" nuclear fuel and both require and produce plutonium. A peculiar problem with plutonium, besides its extraordinary toxicity, is its immediate accessibility for constructing nuclear weapons. For a nation that has either breeder reactors or a reprocessing plant, the process of diversion and weapons construction could be so rapid that the international community would have no "time-buffer," or interval in which to react diplomatically or take protective measures. (And the opportunities for theft by terrorists would be correspondingly enhanced—though somewhat impaired by the high radioactivity of the stolen materials.)

A major gap has opened up between the United States, on one side, and certain European countries (notably France and Germany) and Japan, on the other, on the subject of nuclear fuel, with the latter countries claiming a need for proceeding with breeder reactors because of uncertainties of supplies of both conventional fuels and enriched uranium. A further strain arises from the efforts of energy-poor third world countries, such as Brazil and Pakistan, to shield their sovereignty and secure their economies from future external pressures by acquiring the technologies for extracting plutonium from nuclear wastes.

A possible way out of some of these dilemmas is promised by the "International Fuel Cycle Evaluation" (IFCE), inaugurated in 1977 as a cooperative effort by 44 nations and international institutions to study "proliferation-resistant" fuel technologies, and to suggest ways to secure the entire fuel cycle and manage spent fuel and nuclear wastes. The temporary banning and early superseding of plutonium by denatured or alternative and safer fuels would seem to be the most urgent task in the control of nuclear proliferation.

Other specific moves that have been proposed by the Carter administration to control, monitor, regulate, or retard the proliferation of nuclear weapons technology include improved "reliability" of nuclear fuel supply through an international nuclear fuel bank (with substantial donations of enriched uranium by the United States); provision of storage facilities within the United States for limited amounts of foreign spent fuel; and regional nuclear fuel reprocessing centers.

But there are problems. As one commentator put it: "There are some big ideas that are not very good and some good ideas that are not very big."*

Safeguards for the entire global nuclear fuel cycle could have implications that would be very restrictive for the kinds of civil liberties—particularly freedom of movement, freedom from search and surveillance—to which we have become accustomed, at least as attainable ideals. Assuring the rest of the world of continuous and adequate supplies of nuclear fuel—through shipments of original enriched uranium as well as reprocessed nuclear materials—might put rigid restrictions on America's political and commercial behavior and commit us to supporting many unpalatable regimes. Offering to store indefinitely the world's nuclear wastes within our own territory (their period of serious radioactivity can be as long as 250,000 years) presents the specter of an unmanageable immediate political problem as well as an eventual environmental disaster.

The very nature of nuclear materials (whether military or "peaceful") defies a single analogy: Are they a plague or a tool? A poison or an instrument? Unfortunately, they have elements of both. A certain degree of ambivalence is just a recognition of the problem. But this much must be said: Failure to find reasonably safe nuclear fuels and to perfect (or eliminate) waste disposal must halt the further installation of nuclear systems.

No one can prescribe completely satisfactory controls on nuclear weapons and nuclear materials—or avoid completely the task of devising them. No nation can confidently implicate itself in international political regimes to determine other nations' acquisition and use of nuclear arms and materials—or completely escape from the consequences of other nations' malfeasance.

We advocate the practical moves described above and the setting of an example by the restrained conduct of the United States; but we would avoid either forcible measures to restrain other countries or the extension of nuclear guarantees and other military commitments to secure their compliance in a regime of non-proliferation.

13. Conventional War: Arms Transfers and Regional Agreements

With regard to conventional arms, there has been more prescription than analysis, more solutions than definitions of the problem. We have to begin by asking why there is a problem, and whose problem it is—what is the cause and what is the effect.

Three troublesome aspects present themselves on the surface of the situation:

1. The entire world, in the aggregate, now diverts close to $400 billion dollars of resources a year to the production and purchase of arms. Of this total, almost $25 billion represents arms transfers.* And of these arms transfers, it is estimated that developing nations receive two-thirds. Obviously, even a small portion of these aggregate amounts could go far toward solving desperate problems of poverty, disease, malnutrition, inadequate housing, illiteracy, agricultural deficiency, and urban decay.

2. Countries such as the United States are

Though the arms suppliers are actively peddling, the arms recipients are also actively shopping, for purposes that they themselves insist on determining.

shipping arms that become instruments of repression by dictatorial, reactionary regimes.

3. The major arms suppliers are fueling regional arms races that might erupt in war; and the sophisticated and extremely lethal arms that are supplied make those wars more intense and destructive, and more expensive, than they might otherwise have been. (The 1973 war in the Middle East, for example, supposedly cost a billion dollars a day.)

The implication in many discussions of this problem is that the major arms suppliers (the United States, the USSR, Britain, and France, which together supply more than 80 percent of military exports) are, for their own selfish purposes (employment, balance of payments, regional influence and control), pushing unwanted and unnecessarily large quantities of these sophisticated and lethal arms on countries that can hardly resist the pressures and otherwise would not make the decision to acquire them. Though the purposes of the suppliers (give or take a few adjectives) are accurately described, the situation is different with respect to the recipients. Though the arms suppliers are actively peddling, the arms recipients are also actively shopping, for purposes that they themselves insist on determining. Further, the fact that some of the purposes of the arms recipients, whether valid or not, are at least not trivial complicates the problem of controlling the transfer of arms.

In fact, certain trends in arms transfers over

---

*Daniel Yergin, "The Limits of Non-Proliferation," *The New Republic*, January 22, 1977.

*In 1976 arms expenditures were estimated at over $350 billion (Ruth Leger Sivard, *World Military and Social Expenditures*, 1977 edition, Leesburg, Virginia: WMSE Publications, 1977). On May 19, 1977, President Carter reported that "total arms sales in recent years have risen to over $20 billion" (*Department of State Bulletin*, June 13, 1977, p. 625).

the past decade have made the problem even more elusive:

1. The bulk of the transfers has changed from grants to sales (even though concessive credit is still much used and the sales are handled largely through official, rather than purely commercial, channels).

2. There is more straight business—as opposed to political—competition among suppliers, even within the West (the United States, Britain, France, and to some extent West Germany, Italy, and others—even Israel).

3. Wealthy oil-producing nations in the third world (prominently Iran and Saudi Arabia) have the wherewithal to pay for sophisticated, first-line military equipment. Correspondingly, the arms suppliers (who are also net oil consumers) have a need to balance their oil deficits with higher levels of military sales.

4. There is increasing indigenous production of arms, including major items of equipment such as aircraft, among recipient countries; and there are often co-production arrangements with the supplier nations. In some cases (India, Israel, even Brazil), local arms industries have exportable surpluses. "Third country" sales are becoming an increasing problem, complicating efforts, such as supplier conferences, to limit competition for arms sales.

In the area of conventional arms transfers, just as in the area of nuclear proliferation, we need overlapping, not necessarily neat or comprehensive, efforts. First, we should seek supplier agreements to limit arms infusions into regions, according to overall volume and kinds of weapons.

The expression of a serious intent by the United States to cut back on arms production for export would have to be underscored and validated by a program of conversion of defense industry, and compensation, retraining, and relocation of displaced defense workers.

There have also been suggestions for a more comprehensive multilateral control of arms transfers. In one scheme,* a United Nations agency would collect information on each country's military spending, set standards, measure the excess or shortfall, and establish certain incentives (such as participation in a special development assistance fund, to be raised by assessing a tax on nations that exceeded their standard) to encourage nations to cut their military expenditures including arms imports. This sort of measure, though ingenious and appealing, seems needlessly complicated. The "opportunity costs" of arms spending are all too painfully clear without tying development assistance explicitly to military frugality. And the subject of arms reductions is already too complex and contentious without creating further linkages, which themselves would have to be debated and might then stall the progress of disarmament itself. Peace and lower arms expenditures will have to be their own reward for nations that choose them. Decisions about what to do with the "surplus" will have to be resolved within the political processes of nations, but in a separate and independent stage.

The primary and the ultimate condition for stopping the importation of arms into a region will remain the absence or lessening of political-military competition within the region. In turn, the motives and compulsions of the regional countries will have to be addressed, causally. The recipients will continue to demand arms as long as their security, nation by nation, appears to be threatened by neighbors (however reciprocal, circular, and absurd the process).

As for the arms suppliers, there are both external and internal motivations. They will continue to manufacture and attempt to dispose of arms as long as they see some point in securing political and strategic benefits—regional influence, control—through arms sales. In some cases, it might even be true that arms sales at a certain controlled level might stabilize a regional contest or benignly influence a recipient nation's policies or actions. For supplier nations, therefore, to accept general restraints on arms transfers, they would have to weigh and accept some disadvantages in the short run, in the hope that the longer-run consequences of a consistent policy of restraint would be more advantageous.

Internally, suppliers will not significantly limit arms transfers as long as employment in important geographical and industrial sectors—and therefore political support—appears to depend on this production. That is why the expression of a serious intent by the United States to cut back on arms production for export would have to be underscored and validated by a program of conversion of defense industry, and compensation, retraining, and relocation of displaced defense workers. Several such proposals have been aired in the past decade (the principal ones associated with the sponsorship of Senator George McGovern and the analysis of Seymour Melman). These should be considered seriously and soon. (There is even an Office of Economic Adjustment in the Pentagon, in existence since 1961, but with a staff of only about 20, to assist "Anytown, USA, suffering economic reversals directly or indirectly due to changes in Defense Programs." This

---

*Lincoln P. Bloomfield and Harlan Cleveland, *The UN Special Session on Disarmament: A "Shadow" Strategy for the United States* (DRAFT), Aspen Institute for Humanistic Studies, November 25, 1977, pp. 43, 44 ff.

office has dealt with finding money within present Federal programs to channel into communities hurt by base closures, to transfer defense department property to communities, and to help people find alternative employment. This kind of activity has to be broadened.)

President Carter, in his May 1977 statement, purported to enunciate a new policy of restraint in arms transfers. He put forward several criteria of control: dollar volume, advanced weapons, sophisticated weapons, co-production, re-export. The themes of his program were that "the United States will henceforth view arms transfers as an exceptional foreign policy implement, to be used only in instances where it can be clearly demonstrated that the transfer contributes to our national security interests"; and "in the future the burden of persuasion will be on those who favor a particular arms sale rather than those who oppose it." Along with the innuendo that the preceding administration had done much the opposite, these pronouncements make a distinction without a difference. Moreover, in the subsequent history of this administration's practice, the "new" arms transfer policy has been honored more in the breach than the observance. U.S. foreign military sales in FY 1978, the first full year of this administration's control of the program, are rising to $13.2 billion, compared with $11.2 billion in FY 1977.

To reverse this trend, an American administration would have to believe that the United States cannot have a general long-term interest in a world of increasingly heavily armed autonomous nations, or a world in which the United States is tied increasingly to the policies and actions—and their consequences and outcomes—of its particular clients. An attack on the problem of conventional arms proliferation can begin only in the abstention by each supplier nation from the transfer of any direct implements of war. Such a principle of national self-denial should be adopted by our own country, and in applying the principle we should fear its overqualification more than its overgeneralization.

14. Confidence-Building and Peace-Keeping

If we are serious about improving the incentives for nations not to arm, threaten war, wage war, overprepare for war, or escalate to nuclear war, we must provide more reliable mechanisms for promoting each nation's confidence in others' intentions, settling disputes, and interposing peace-keeping forces between contestants.

There are also larger changes that must be brought about in the style of international policies. In the present "game" of employing force economically in balance-of-power situations, some theorists advocate the cultivation of ambiguity, purposely keeping the other side in a state of uncertainty

---

Some theorists advocate the cultivation of ambiguity, purposely keeping the other side in a state of uncertainty about one's own intentions. This kind of behavior will lead to a more precarious and ultimately more expensive, as well as risky, world.

---

about one's own intentions. This kind of behavior will lead to a more precarious and ultimately more expensive, as well as risky, world.

It would be otiose here to do more than indicate some of the measures and concrete institutions for confidence-building, since this has been one of the more developed areas of peace planning in the past several decades. Confidence-building measures include, or would include, warning of troop movements, notice of test firings of missiles, exchange of information on weapons systems and military budgets, inspection devices and joint teams at missile sites, "hot lines" and other communications systems, agreements not to interfere with others' observation satellites in space, and various crisis monitoring and predicting networks.

One of the more successful and mutually acceptable portions of the Helsinki Accords of August 1975, which culminated the Conference on Security and Cooperation in Europe (CSCE), was the section on confidence-building measures. And, in general, two of the more promising kinds of controls on war and escalation are: (1) prevention of misinterpretations of intentions, when nations in fact do not intend war or escalation (this is "confidence-building" in the strict sense); and (2) where pairs of nations do intend harm to one another, the speedy interposition of outside influence, to limit damage, damp down the intensity of the quarrel, and above all seal it off so that it does not spread, via allies, suppliers, and sympathetic nations, to other geographical areas.

The latter function is "peace-keeping." In this function, despite disillusion and skepticism about international organizations in the role of authoritative world governments or true regimes of collective security, the United Nations has had considerable success. It is important to realize, however, that peace-keeping, unlike true collective security, does not put a complete safety net under the international system. Measures of peace-keeping, conciliation, and interposition have to be distinguished (as by Secretary-General U Thant in 1963) from the prior UN emphasis on opposing aggression. Differences are present on all dimensions: in peace-keeping there is no identification of an "aggressor," indeed no presumption of aggression; no taking of sides; no use of lethal or other forcible means unless directly provoked or attacked by one of the parties; and no use of large, powerful nations for police duty.

In this area of peace-keeping the United Nations promises to have both a continuing role, even in a considerably disarmed world, and considerable success, since both the United States and the Soviet Union appear to have a cooperative interest in damping down and containing regional crises (the attitude of China and, in certain other cases, other veto-bearing members of the UN Security Council is somewhat more doubtful). This is true even though each power might obstruct UN action where it sees possible gain for a regional proxy, up to the point where it incurs dangers to itself.

Peace-keeping is a vital function in any scheme of disarmament. It is one of the conditions for creating sufficient incentives for the disarmament of the larger powers, the present "guarantors." They must have the assurance that a local conflict will be contained short of the point where they would "have to" become involved. That kind of confidence, provided by a supranational organization or mechanism, is one of the specific trade-offs necessary to induce the dismantling of the present opposing military alliance systems. Those alliance systems, in their present form and concept, attempt to deter conflicts precisely by threatening to escalate and expand them.

But even peace-keeping presents certain problems: We must be careful that interpositions of external influence, in the name of "peace-keeping," do not turn into coercive intrusions into the business of individual nations. We must not lose sight of the purpose of peace-keeping—to make the international system freer from "outside" intrusions of force, to keep conflicts localized, and to make the world more compartmentalized in a political-military sense.

Peace-keeping, as an effective process and as a general rule of action, could, however, cut across the thrust for justice, for the satisfaction of the aspirations of nations and peoples still submerged and oppressed. For peace-keeping must be relatively blind to the respective merits of the causes in a quarrel. Thus, the questions are raised: how to accommodate political change? how to reconcile peace and justice? Specifically, what about the several residual anti-colonial struggles, particularly in southern Africa? And further, what about the contest, just beginning, between the "South" and the "North," and the force which, put behind the claims of the have-not nations for a "new international economic order"— for a "fairer" dispensation of the world's raw materials, productive resources, and technology— might make such claims more than contemptible?

Obviously, the conflicting claims of peace and justice have to be balanced. An emphasis on the control of conflict might induce more agnosticism about the claims of "justice" than we might otherwise afford. The principle of simply containing conflict might, in some cases, be morally bleak. But there is a thought that might go toward mitigating any apparent bias in favor of peace and against justice: Compartmentalizing conflict (through supranational peace-keeping combined with national policies of non-intervention) might even provide a series of bulkheads within the international system, and thus allow overall order—the urgently required super-stability of the entire international system in a nuclear age—to coexist with the possibility of sharp and rough change within the components of the system.

15. War Crimes and Personal Accountability

In considering incentives to go to war or escalate the level of war, there will be no lasting progress until responsibility—particularly for nuclear war (the mass targeting of nuclear weapons, the execution of a first nuclear strike)—is fixed at the level of the genesis of all human action: the will and the conscience of the individual person.

This emphasis on strict morality and legal responsibility reverses the ethical vogue of the past thirty years or so, a vogue remarkably coincident with the cold war . . .

This does not imply a theory that pathologies of the individual are the unique, or even the principal, determinant of war. Social and political structures, the play of collective objectives and constraints, and the shape of the international system might be more potent influences on human action. Indeed, the attempt to fix responsibility presumes rational control by individuals of their own actions, even where, in fact, one could deduce "sickness" for the conduct itself. In short, we are not trying to substitute psychology for morality, criminology for law. Quite the contrary, individual responsibility is the presumption that makes international law possible. Every significant advance in the international law of war has involved a sharpening of the sense of the criminality of various practices and the responsibility of the individual for his actions, despite the invention of exculpatory devices such as the claim of compulsion of superior authority.

This emphasis on strict morality and legal responsibility reverses the ethical vogue of the past thirty years or so, a vogue remarkably coincident with the cold war: the two-tier ethic of statecraft, the

Niebuhrian double standard, associated with the "realists," the exponents of the balance of power and the national interest. This two-tier ethic postulates one realm for the individual (traditional Christian morality) and another for the statesman (an amoral world, validated in the pronouncements of ethicists, political scientists, and statesmen themselves, who wish for a reprieve from the ordinary definition of words and the ordinary judgment of actions). The culmination of this thrust has been undeclared wars, covert political actions, assassinations, destabilizations of lawful and popular regimes, secrecy in government, deception of citizens, and arrogation of egregious war powers by the Executive.

All that has to be reversed. We have to return to the tradition of the Nuremberg Trials and the inhibitions on the initiation of war codified in the United Nations Charter and, before that, the Kellogg-Briand Treaty of 1928, outlawing aggressive war. We have to pay more than patronizing lip-service to the notion of morally binding codes of statecraft.

In the nation-state system that will prevail for the foreseeable future, it will be up to citizens to enforce their best standards and values upon their own statesmen—unevenly, to be sure, because of the unevenness of political opportunity across the world—but enforce nonetheless. Citizens must stop being deluded into thinking that license granted differentially to their own statesmen will lead to national advantages. The ideals that we claim to be at the foundation of our nation must be asserted again in our nation's practices—not for some ulterior, presumably strategic, good but for our own ultimate good. (In addition, in a "Kantian" fashion, the extension of such moral principles more universally would conduce to a more benign international system, from a political and strategic standpoint.)

Certain concrete moves should be taken. There exist already, both as codified law, in some cases awaiting ratification, and in other cases as drafts and proposals ripe for official and popular consideration, statutes on war crimes and accountability.

A salient example is the proposed "Official Accountability Act," first introduced to Congress in 1973 as H.R. 8388, and subjected to hearings in the House on February 2, 1976, before the Subcommittee on Courts, Civil Liberties, and the Administration of Justice, of the Committee on the Judiciary. Though the hearings disclosed some defects—such as the incorporation by vague reference of international law and custom instead of delineating crimes—and kinks in language and procedure, the thrust of this legislation is mind-bending and crucial to a strategy of disarmament. It would be revolutionary if adopted even in one country.

As Chairman Robert Kastenmeier put it: "The basic notion [of this bill is] that a nation's political leaders should be held personally accountable for criminal acts committed at their command . . . by

---

We have to return to the tradition of the Nuremberg Trials and the inhibitions on the initiation of war codified in the United Nations Charter and, before that, the Kellogg-Briand Treaty of 1928, outlawing aggressive war. We have to pay more than patronizing lip-service to the notion of morally binding codes of statecraft.

---

incorporating the international laws and customs of war, to which this Nation already subscribes, into the Federal Criminal Code, and by establishing an institutional mechanism for the investigation and prosecution of violations of those laws."

The bill encompasses such crimes as: "the planning of, preparation for, initiation or waging of a war of aggression or a war in violation of any international treaty or agreement to which the United States is a party," "any violation of the laws and customs of war . . . murdering, torturing, using as hostages, using for slave labor . . . any prisoners of war or any civilians of another nation . . . wantonly destroying cities, towns, or villages," and "bombing of civilian populations for the purpose of terrorizing such civilian populations" (a clause that has implications for the use of nuclear weapons, because of the intrinsically indiscriminate nature of these weapons); and also "overthrowing by force, violence, or bribery the leadership of a nation with which the United States is not at war" (a provision that has obvious relation to covert operations).

It goes on to set criminal penalties for such infractions—imprisonment of two to 25 years or alternative expiation through restitutive civilian work—and also prescribes, as an alternative or additional penalty, ineligibility for employment by the United States for a period of fifteen years. It proposes that a special Solicitor, in charge of investigating and prosecuting such crimes, have the right to seek "preventive relief, including a permanent or temporary injunction, restraining order, or such other order as he deems necessary," and "render advisory opinions on the legality . . . of any proposed action with respect to which such opinion is requested." Periodic public hearings are specified, to collect evidence of infractions.

Give or take some argument about the appropriateness of sentences and perhaps the administrative and judicial procedures for apprehension and conviction, this legislation should be brought to the surface of public and official debate and introduced into our statute books—both for our own sake and as an example and a goal for other nations.

There is some question as to whether such an investigative and even prosecutorial agency should have international or transnational character. An agency called the "International Disarmament Organization" was proposed in the U.S. and Soviet disarmament drafts of 1962, with powers to operate in this area of criminal procedure. The question is whether its actions should be binding within national jurisdictions. A truly pervasive international enforcement organization might put the whole matter of accountability beyond practicability. In fact, it might not even be an improvement, unless it is assumed that other nations' practices are superior to our own standards and values (whether honored in the observance or the breach).

War crimes and official accountability are not the only aspects of this problem of internalizing civilized standards of national behavior. War-prone behavior and tendencies to criminal actions in war can also be curtailed by other mechanisms, which should be given the most serious attention. This opens up a whole area of non-governmental actions that can be accomplished by transnational groups of citizens, such as professional associations, religious denominations, and educational organizations. There could be such moves as registries of scientists doing military research, and pledges by scientists not to engage in work on weapons systems that are intended, or limited by their nature, to perpetrating aggressive or genocidal war; oaths by military personnel not to fight immoral or aggressive wars; some shift in the legal burdens relating to selective tax avoidance, the refusal to commit personal resources to destructive national uses; and the development of course materials for schools, suggesting moral presumptions restrictive of arms accumulation and war.

The point is that a significant part of the thrust to fix personal responsibility for war and war crimes lies just outside the ambit of purely legal restriction. It consists of the arousal of citizen concern for the behavior of their leaders; political support for restraints on official action, including pressures on congresspersons to raise these issues; and even the penetration of bureaucracies, reaching the consciences of individual office-holders and ultimately affecting the "ethos" of the bureaus involved in preparing for wars.

16. General and Complete Disarmament

A serious program of arms limitation must move toward the goal of general and complete disarmament. A starting point—in fact, the point where the disarmament process seems to have left off—is the September 1961 McCloy-Zorin "Joint Statement of Agreed Principles" and the 1962 draft treaties by the United States and the Soviet Union for general and complete disarmament. In reviewing the American draft, "Outline of Basic Provisions of a Treaty on General and Complete Disarmament in a Peaceful World," presented by the United States to the Eighteen-Nation Committee on Disarmament on April 18, 1962, and the corresponding Soviet draft, we should take note of several elements that seem usable in a new regime of disarmament, some points on which the parties had differing approaches, and a few proposals that might be troublesome in constructing an agreement appropriate to our times:

● The agreement is phased, and provides for three stages, with a pause for verification and the gaining of confidence before proceeding to the next stage. This principal is essential—though (1) a time-

A serious program of arms limitation must move toward the goal of general and complete disarmament.

table in itself doesn't make the program more realistic, and (2) our conception of a phased program includes independent national initiatives as well as bilateral and multilateral agreements.

● Nuclear and conventional arms, production, development, research, military budgets, conscription, and training are all encompassed and considered to be linked. This principle must also be retained in any contemporary formulation.

● Access is established for some supranational or cross-national inspection teams, to verify compliance. This principle, asserted by the United States and accepted by the Soviet Union, appears essential.

● Both sides postulate an "International Disarmament Organization," that would have certain verification, inspection and informational duties, without having enforcement powers. This is entirely sensible, and would be the minimal basis for continuing confidence by the nations involved.

● Chemical and biological as well as nuclear weapons are marked for progressive dismantling and destruction. This principle should be maintained in any new agreement.

● United Nations mechanisms for the peaceful settlement of disputes are strengthened. This, too, seems an essential condition for individual nations to attenuate their arms.

● All drafts attempt to preserve military balance over the stages of disarmament, so that no state might achieve strategic advantage. This is also a principle that must be retained in any agreement (though it is easy to see how this generally sensible principle could be made so meticulous and rigid that it would constitute an obstacle to agreement).

● Troops of all nations are to be withdrawn from foreign military deployment, and bases in the territory of other nations are to be dismantled. These provisions can be adopted in the early stages of a program of disarmament.

● Nuclear weapons and the means of delivery are a subject of divergence in the U.S. and Soviet drafts. Both proposals envisage the ultimate elimination of nuclear weapons, down to zero. But the Soviet draft specifies that nuclear weapons, except for a "limited number" of ICBMs, are to be dismantled in the first stage, and the remainder in the second stage; while the U.S. draft specifies a 30 percent cut in all categories of arms, nuclear and conventional, in the first stage, another 35 percent in Stage II, and the remainder in the final Stage III. The point is clear. In the U.S. draft, if Stage III were never reached, some nuclear weapons, as well as, of course, other kinds, would be retained. If all nuclear (and perhaps near-nuclear) states were included in the disarmament agreement, then perhaps something approximating the Soviet provision for first- and second-stage elimination would be superior (give or take a more balanced inventory of types of delivery vehicles). But if significant nuclear states (such as China) remained outside this disarmament agreement, and it were still regarded as advantageous for the United States and the Soviet Union to enter into an essentially bilateral agreement (though perhaps with other adherents), then it is not hard to see why the U.S. formulation might have to be the norm. (Another problem with the proposals for nuclear elimination is that most present nuclear states could assemble new nuclear weapons quickly, virtually from scratch.)

What we are talking about is a system of disarmament that would be essentially *unenforced*. This should not be taken on its face as unrealistic. Though it requires an act of imagination, it is simply an expression of the kind of world that can be predicted for the next fifty years or so, at least.

● At the end of the disarmament process, a supranational United Nations agency is postulated as the sole remaining repository of forces and weapons that could be used with significant international effect—that is, for more than local or border defense. This would be an agency, in the words of the U.S. draft, that would have "sufficient armed forces and armaments so that no state could challenge it" (p. 307). Of course, the U.S. and the Soviet drafts favored different constitutions for these peace forces. The Soviet Union suggested a force with the command "composed of the three principal groups of States existing in the world on the basis of equal representation" (p. 327); while the United States envisaged a composition arising from Article 43 of the UN Charter (p. 296). But the main point is that such a reliable global police force is the condition that unlocks the final stage of any disarmament agreement—the stage when nations give up the last substance of their effective military forces. (Conversely, this global peace force depends on the existence of a disarmed world.) Therefore, for this precise reason, provisions for such a force, just as provision for the final stage of disarmament, would be subject to substantial revision in an agreement appropriate to the predictable international climate of the next half century. (This judgment does not preclude the convening of the UN military committee specified in Article 43 of the Charter; but its role would be directed more to formulating aspects of a world disarmament plan from the standpoint of the technical requirements of military security and balance.)

What we are talking about is a system of disarmament that would be essentially *unenforced.* This should not be taken on its face as unrealistic. Though it requires an act of imagination, it is simply an expression of the kind of world that can be predicted for the next fifty years or so, at least. It might be tempting to "solve" this problem by designing structures of world government and mechanisms of supranational enforcement. But that would be simply to substitute one kind of imagination for another. And that is precisely what has been wrong with previous proposals of disarmament. Moreover, it is hard to see how other ingenious kinds of measures, such as the forfeiture of performance bonds, or the more traditional kinds of sanctions (communications disruption, economic embargo) would be any more feasible than global police forces. All suffer from the probable lack of an unarguable central agency to dictate and implement enforcement. One kind of recourse, since we are not thinking of enforcement by a centralized coercive authority, would be to nongovernmental groups—transnational organizations, that would operate, however, essentially through the legal systems of each country (even if such operation would be uneven across the spectrum of states). Such organizations would reinforce the extension of international law within nation-states; they could formulate new laws, monitor the compliance of leaders, expose violations, and bring actions in national courts against their own statesmen.

● The final stage of disarmament (Stage III) provides for virtually complete dismantling of all military forces, weapons, vehicles, means of arms production, launching sites, staging and training areas, barracks, command structures, conscription, and military budgets—either their elimination, transfer to a supranational organization, or conversion to non-military use. The only kinds of forces that are to survive the last stage of general and complete disarmament are (in the Soviet draft) "strictly limited contingents of police (militia), equipped with light firearms, to maintain internal order, including the safeguarding of frontiers and the personal security of citizens, and to provide for compliance with their obligations in regard to the maintenance of international peace and security under the United Nations Charter" (p. 326); while the U.S. draft provides: "States would have at their disposal only those non-nuclear armaments, forces, facilities and establishments as are agreed to be necessary to maintain internal order and protect the personal security of citizens" (p. 280).

An appropriate contemporary agreement, more skeptical of substituting universal means of preserving world order, would have to allow correspondingly higher numbers of residual forces or a more permissive definition of the forces "necessary to maintain internal order," "the safeguarding of frontiers," etc.

Nothing is said in the American and Soviet drafts about military alliances (except for the dismantling of foreign bases and the end of foreign troop deployments), though in a very real sense military alliances are a transmission belt and an amplification system for war. Obviously, associations among nations that are now directed to military purposes, even if they survived, would have to be transformed. At first, certain treaty organizations such as NATO and the Warsaw Pact could be given quasi-collaborative and quasi-negotiating tasks, such as working out regional arms reduction plans and inspection arrangements. In the process, they would at least acquire the habit of working cooperatively, and they might ultimately take the form of joint military commissions to provide for regional collective security. Other military alliance organizations, such as CENTO, are less obviously useful in these purposes, and should be dismantled. SEATO has already been scrapped.

From the foregoing discussion we can distill some general "guidelines" for a treaty on general and complete disarmament:

☐ The end-point has to be acceptable in a climate of multiple, independent nation-states; it must take account of their true minimum defensive needs, without assuming the existence of a global UN police force or the assurance of appeal to an effective international tribunal with the power to adjudicate and enforce.

☐ Each point in a phased process has to be stable, from the standpoint of the incentives of opposing, or at least not entirely harmonious, political entities. Some measures of disarmament—some simple reductions in numbers and types of weapons—can be destabilizing. A concern for stability might well create a "jagged line," rather than a straight orthogenetic path, from the present superabundance of arms to effective disarmament.

☐ The phases should be set in finite time, but not so rigidly that the time intervals themselves become a point of contention; though also not so loosely that the proposals can be regarded as nothing but utopian ideals. The sequence of phases could take ten or fifteen years.

☐ Pauses and checkpoints have to be provided for evaluation of progress, verification of compliance, and the gaining of confidence in the moves of the prior stage. The indices used for verification should not be so obscure that they become meaningless or contentious. Verification should hinge on obvious and identifiable criteria, even if they are somewhat mechanical.

☐ Disarmament moves should be taken for the purpose of peace and stability and the reduction of the burdens of arms expenditures, without complicating them with explicit linkages involving reallocation of savings to other functional areas, such as development. Such other purposes may be entirely valid, but should be proposed separately, on their own merits. Of course, the point is not lost that savings from reduced military expenditures—and they would be very large—are available for other, more worthy and more pressing, human needs and social requirements. But tight and explicit reallocation would create another set of contentious and complex issues and possibly stall the disarmament negotiations themselves.

☐ There has to be room for independent initiatives, taken by individual nations for their own prudent purposes, to reduce the risks and burdens of military postures and doctrines. The independent moves (such as eliminating fixed land-based missiles, no first use of nuclear weapons, large cuts in conventional forces, attenuation of military alliances) have to be accommodated in a comprehensive framework and methodology, along with the more formal bilateral or multilateral disarmament negotiations. There should be provision for verification of these independent moves by the other side. Independent initiatives would function to create momentum for the disarmament process and break deadlocks at critical points; to indicate the scope of possibilities that are achievable; and to generate public and even elite support, transforming the climate in which disarmament might proceed. The insistence on independent moves within a framework of comprehensive disarmament is not a contradiction, but a frank recognition of reality and actually an unconditional commitment to progress in arms reductions and war avoidance. We want the substance of disarmament, in any way it can be achieved.

The ultimate goal, that infuses these proposals with vitality and coherence, is a new kind of international order and a new mode of American conduct. In disarmament and in non-intervention lie true national and world security.

Other Institute Publications

Chile:
Economic 'Freedom' and Political Repression
by Orlando Letelier
This in-depth analysis by a former leading official of the Allende government of Chile demonstates the necessary relationship between an economic development model which benefits only a rich minority and the political terror which has reigned in Chile since the overthrow of the Allende regime. $.50.

The International Economic Order, Part 1
by Orlando Letelier and Michael Moffitt
The pamphlet traces historically the conflict between the advanced capitalist countries and the Third World over the establishment of a "new international economic order." Special attention is paid to the role of the U.N., the Non-aligned movement, and OPEC. $3.00.

The Crisis of the Corporation
by Richard Barnet
The pamphlet describes the power of the multinational corporations which dominate the U.S. economy. Barnet shows how the growth of multinationals inevitably results in an extreme concentration of economic and political power in a few hands. The result, according to Barnet, is a crisis for democracy itself. $1.50.

The New Gnomes:
Multinational Banks in the Third World
by Howard M. Wachtel
The pamphlet documents and analyzes the growth of Third World debt by private U.S.-based multinational banks and the impact of this new form of indebtedness on the politics and economic policies of Third World countries. $3.00.

Special Report:
Black South Africa Explodes
by Counter Information Services, London
Black South Africa Explodes is the only detailed account of events in South Africa in the first year since the uprising which began in June, 1976, in Soweto. The report exposes the reality of life in the African townships, the impact of South Africa's economic crisis on blacks, and the white regime's dependence on European and American finance. $2.00.

Human Rights and Vital Needs
by Peter Weiss
This speech was delivered one year after the assassination of Orlando Letelier and Ronni Karpen Moffitt in Washington, D.C. This extraordinary address weaves the commemoration of Letelier and Moffitt with a broadening definition of human rights, demanding that the U.S. include economic, social and cultural rights along with political and civil rights in our human rights policy. $.50.

The Federal Budget and Social Reconstruction
Marcus Raskin, Editor in Chief
Where the tax money goes and where it comes from have long been obscured in the fog of numbers that keeps the public from understanding or controlling the budget-making and taxing processes—the heart of politics. At the request of 54 members of Congress, and as an attempt to demystify the budget-making process, the Institute has published this collection of 21 papers on alternative policies for spending on defense, energy, housing, health, unemployment and inflation, public enterprise, etc. Included are some unique ideas on tax reform and balancing the federal budget. $7.95. **Your Money and Your Life** (condensed version of **The Federal Budget Study and Social Reconstruction**), $1.95.

The Counterforce Syndrome:
A Guide to U.S. Nuclear Weapons and Strategic Doctrine
by Robert C. Aldridge
The pamphlet identifies how "counterforce" has replaced "deterrence" as the Pentagon's prevailing doctrine, contrary to what most Americans believe. Aldridge, a former Lockheed engineer, offers a thorough summary and analysis of U.S. strategic nuclear weapons and military doctrine. A discussion of the U.S. nuclear arsenal of MIRVs, MARVs, Trident systems, cruise missiles, and M-X missiles describes these weapons as they relate to the aim of a U.S. first strike. $2.50.

World Hunger: Causes and Remedies
An article based on part one of a Transnational Institute Report prepared for presentation at the United Nations World Food Conference in Rome in November, 1974. $2.50.

Supplying Repression:
U.S. Support for Authoritarian Regimes Abroad
by Michael T. Klare
This pamphlet describes how the U.S. continues to supply arms and training to police and other internal security forces of repressive governments abroad. $2.50.

Dubious Specter:
A Second Look at the Soviet 'Threat'
by Fred M. Kaplan
Introduction by Richard J. Barnet
The pamphlet is a thorough and convincing exposition and analysis of the myths and realities surrounding the current U.S.-Soviet "military balance." With careful documentation, Kaplan refutes claims of Soviet military superiority expounded by Paul Nitze, Richard Pipes and others of the Committee on the Present Danger. His comparisons of U.S. and Soviet nuclear arsenals and strategies provide the necessary background for understanding current debates on arms limitations and rising military costs. $2.50.

Whistle-Blower's Guide to the Federal Bureaucracy
by Government Accountability Project, IPS
This handbook was written as an aid to employees of the federal government who need to reach the public with evidence of illegal or improper practices by their agencies. Based on the experience of veteran whistle-blowers such as Ernie Fitzgerald, it tells prospective whistle-blowers what consequences they might expect, and how to blow the whistle so as to afford themselves maximum protection. $3.00.

The Ford Report
by Counter Information Services, London
The latest "anti-report" by CIS, a London affiliate of IPS's Transnational Institute, is a comprehensive and well-documented study on the Ford Motor Company. Just published, *The Ford Report* deals with Ford activities in South Africa, Ford's role in the Common Market, Ford's plans for the Third World, wages and working conditions, death on the job, profits and production, and Ford's blueprint for the future. $2.50.

Postage and Handling:

All orders should include postage. For single orders add .40; for 10 items, add .75; for 25 items, add $1.75; for 50 items, add $2.00. Orders will be sent book rate, unless otherwise requested. Quantity discounts are available.

$2.00

Institute for Policy Studies

1901 Que Street, N.W.
Washington, D.C. 20009
Tel: 202·234·9382
Cable: IPSWASH, Washington, D.C.

Paulus Potterstraat 20
Amsterdam 1007, Holland
Tel: (020) 72 66 08
Cable: TRANSNAT, Amsterdam